THE LAND LOOKS AFTER US

THE LAND LOOKS AFTER US

A History of Native American Religion

JOEL W. MARTIN

OXFORD
UNIVERSITY PRESS

OXFORD
UNIVERSITY PRESS

Oxford   New York
Athens   Auckland   Bangkok   Bogotá   Buenos Aires   Calcutta
Cape Town   Chennai   Dar es Salaam   Delhi   Florence   Hong Kong
Istanbul   Karachi   Kuala Lumpur   Madrid   Melbourne   Mexico City
Mumbai   Nairobi   Paris   São Paulo   Singapore   Taipei   Tokyo   Toronto
Warsaw   and associated companies in
Berlin   Ibadan

Published by Oxford University Press, Inc.
198 Madison Avenue, New York, New York 10016
www.oup.com

Library of congress cataloging-in-publication data
is available upon request.

ISBN-13: 978-0-19-514586-1
ISBN-10: 0-19-514586-0

9 8 7 6

Printed in the United States of America
on acid-free paper

Design and layout: Casper Grathwohl
Picture research: Lisa Kirchner

Frontispiece: *Lisa Altaha with her godmother during
the Sunrise Dance at the Apache Girls' Puberty Ceremony
at Fort Apache Indian Reservation in Arizona.*

*A significant portion of the author's proceeds
from sales of this book will be donated to support
the work of the Native American Rights Fund,
the American Indian College Fund,
or similar organizations.*

CONTENTS

PREFACE

"Our land, our religion, and our life are one."

Voiced by a Hopi man in 1951, this statement points
to an important truth about his and many other
Native Americans' approaches to the sacred: religion was
not separated from the rest of life. Well before non-Natives
arrived, Native Americans fused spirituality with place and
practice to imbue everyday, local realities with the most profound significance. As a consequence, in North America
there emerged an extraordinary variety of rich, rooted traditions of meaning and power, a first form of North American
religious pluralism. The traditions comprising this
unmatched diversity cultivated an unequaled intimacy with
specific landscapes. These traditions, collectively and indi-
vidually, deserve and reward close attention. They provide
unique perspectives on America. They reveal important
dimensions of spiritual life. They matter.

But representing any one, let alone all, of these traditions adequately in one book is impossible. Because so many
of these traditions were not separated from the rest of life,

one can almost always discern more connections and resonances that need attention. These inclusive, multidimensional traditions infused art and architecture, guided behavior and ceremony, structured social life, and involved men, women, and children in dramas of purpose and renewal, and they still do so for many. If you pull on the thread of "Native American religion," you end up pulling yourself into the study of Native American culture, art, history, economics, music, dance, dress, politics, and almost everything else. Talk about Hopi religion and you must talk about blue corn. One thing always leads to another and another when land, religion, and life "are one."

Because of the variety of Native traditions and the multidimensionality of each of them, this book can represent only a small portion of Native American religious reality. It reflects many careful choices, strategic selections made for the sake of conveying larger truths and correcting common misperceptions. Rather than pretend to cover everything, the book draws on the best of contemporary thinking and writing by Native and non-Native men and women to create a well balanced, trustworthy survey. Some traditions have received more and better scholarly attention than others and this fact influences what the book covers. For example, in the first chapter, which describes how different Native peoples related to specific environments, the Koyukon and Apache peoples' traditions receive close attention not just because they constitute morally impressive systems, but partly because anthropologists Richard Nelson and Keith Basso described them eloquently in their writings.

By the same token, some individual traditions have been misrepresented by non-participants. Many outsiders viewed the Ghost Dance movement as only a last tragic gasp of the Lakotas and assumed that their story ended with the 1890 massacre of

Ghost Dancers at Wounded Knee. Neither assumption was correct. This book retraces the origins of the new religion in
Nevada, its various incarnations, and the diverse responses it
inspired among Native Americans and non-Natives. It also
emphasizes how both the Ghost Dance and the Lakotas continued and changed after Wounded Knee.

Similarly misrepresented are Christian Natives, who are too
often dismissed as inauthentic or depicted only as victims of
colonialism. This book seeks to correct and complicate these
simplistic misunderstandings. It conveys a fuller and more interesting story. Chapter 3, "Native and Christian," describes forced
and voluntary conversion. It traces in close detail how a dream
helped a young Cherokee woman make peace with
Protestantism and find within it symbols, tools, and values useful
to her people. Chapter 3 also provides the spiritual stories of several other individual Christian men and women as well as critical
perspectives on the religion developed by contemporary Native
intellectuals, some of whom castigate Christianity.

Because Chapter 3 deals with Native responses to
Christianity, it functions as a pivotal chapter in this book's organization. It divides the treatment of those indigenous religious
traditions that did not embody significant absorption of
Christianity, from the treatment of those that did. Chapter 2,
"Traditions and Crisis in the Eastern Woodlands," describes
prophetic movements during the colonial period. These sought
to strengthen Native traditions in the context of the
European/American invasion. Visionary leaders critiqued aspects
of European culture, values, and practices. In contrast, Chapter
4, "New Religions in the West," focuses not only on the Ghost
Dance, but also the peyote religion, both of which spread in the
late nineteenth century and presupposed considerable exposure

to and even acceptance of some Christian stories and teachings. This organization supports a historical narrative that provides political context for specific movements and developments. Space and place may matter greatly to Native American traditions, but time and context count too. History affects Native traditions even as Native traditions shape how men and women respond to history.

Throughout, whether treating a movement in the east or west, past or present, the book counters the mistaken ideas that Native Americans and Native American religions did not change. And this book utterly rejects the notion that Native peoples and traditions disappeared because of contact with non-Natives. It shows, instead, that Native peoples have displayed great religious creativity, that their traditions have proved remarkably resilient, and that both have survived—miraculously, unbelievably—in spite of extraordinary challenges. These challenges included horrible diseases, territorial invasion, enslavement, popular and "scientific" expressions of racism, state-enforced dispossession, compulsory conversion to alien ways, separation of children from parents, privation, poverty, isolation, bureaucratic harassment, environmental pollution, unchecked development, tourism, insensitive judicial decisions, and other threats. Many of these negative pressures continue to this very day to take their toll on individuals, communities, and traditions across the country. The book discusses these events, but also examines how Native people overcame colonial horrors and how they resist contemporary forces of destruction. The book shows that spirituality has helped Native men and women enormously across the generations. Prophets gave warriors the courage to fight invaders; peyote worship cured drunkenness; and ceremonial planting of sacred corn helps restore hope to abused women.

Far from romanticizing Native people or their traditions, this book, especially the concluding chapter, discusses the pathologies with which they contend—not always successfully—including alcoholism and drug abuse. The last chapter, however, does sound a hopeful note. Titled "Homecoming," it discerns some positive historical trends, including efforts to revitalize Native languages and reclaim ancestral bones and artifacts. Noting an unprecedented renascence in Native American art, music, and literature, the final chapter points to men and women forging fresh interpretations of what it means to be an Indian in the post-modern urban world. It thus documents a general upswing in the control Indians themselves exercise in representing themselves.

This exciting development—which manifests itself in many areas of society and politics—will likely have profound spiritual repercussions, and not just for Native Americans. As Native Americans seek to reclaim their lands, rights, and power to define themselves, it shapes not just the way they practice and interpret their religious life, but it also affects how non-Natives understand their own identities and envisage their relationship to the past and to America. All Americans—from the oldest first families who appeared here millennia upon millennia ago to the most recent immigrants who arrived yesterday—all, are implicated, like it or not, in a complicated but not yet completed history of contact, conquest, resistance, and possible reconciliation. This may surprise and upset non-Natives who have grown accustomed to defining Indians and Indianness as they like—as disappearing savages, as super-spiritual ecologists, as natural beings, as "Braves" and "Redskins," and so on. Many non-

Natives evidently find themselves threatened when Native Americans reclaim the power to define themselves. They scoff when Native protesters call for professional and collegiate organizations to stop using Indian mascots and icons at sporting events. Or, shocked to find tribes reasserting treaty rights or profiting from modern business enterprises, they forget Native Nations hold unique, sanctioned political status in the United States and charge that contemporary Indians are not "real" Indians. In contrast, some non-Natives respond otherwise, more openly to the complicated legacies imposed by a difficult shared history. They try to rethink who they are, to become more inclusive and self-critical. Learning from the past, they evolve into wiser citizens. Engaging fully with the present, they resolve to build a better foundation for the next generation. The new resurgence of Native Americans thus presents a very positive development, an invitation to everyone to reimagine American history, renew this world, and reinvent local and national identities. This book passes that invitation along to its readers and challenges them to reconsider what "our land," "our religion," and "our life" might mean and can be.

October 2000
Temecula, California

THE LAND LOOKS AFTER US

INDIAN PEOPLES

Makah
Chinook
Salish
Kalapuya
Umpqua
Klamath
Tolowa
Yurok
Modoc
Yuki
Maidu
Pomo
Washo
Miwok
Costanoan

Colville
Spokane
Yakima
Umatilla
Cayuse
Northern
Paiute
Western
Shoshoni
Panamint
Paiute

Kootenai
Kalispel
Coeur
d'Alene
Nez Perce
Shoshoni–
Bannock
Goshute

Blackfeet
Flathead

Gros
Ventre
Crow
Wind River
Shoshoni

Assiniboine
Hidatsa
Mandan
Yanktonai
Arikara
Teton
Sioux
Cheyenne
Yankton
Ponca
Omaha
Pawnee
Arapaho

U t e

Chumash
Chemehuevi
Serrano
Cahuilla
Luiseno
Mojave
Havasupai
Yavapai
Yuma
Papago
Pima

Navajo
Hopi
Zuni
Laguna
Acoma
White
Mountain
Apache
Chiricahua

Jicarilla
Tewa
Tano
Pecos
Mescalero

Kiowa

Comanche

Lipan
Apache

2

This map represents historic and contemporary homelands of some of the hundreds of Native American nations in the United States, 1600–2001.

CHAPTER ONE

Circling Earth

For some American Indians involved in Native American religions, life unfolds as a rich drama. This drama plays out in a world filled with spiritual forces and shaped by them. Everything can mean something. Little is separate from religious influence. Spiritually attuned Native American men and women seek multiple ways to express their religious visions. Their spirituality can affect how they cook, eat, dance, paint, tell stories, mold pottery, dye clothes, decorate their bodies, design their homes, organize their villages, court lovers, marry, bury, dress, speak, make love, cut their hair, and so on. Wisdom comes by paying attention to the living world, discerning the spiritual dimension within it, and debating its significance with others in a community. For people holding this perspective, everyday realities can carry extraordinary significance. Dreams may matter. Mountains can harbor gods. Even practical activities can carry religious meaning. Agriculture can be sacred; hunting holy.

Some Hopis view the world this way. Gifted farmers, they grow corn in the near-desert of northeastern Arizona. For some Hopis, planting and raising corn possesses a spiritual significance. In contemplating it, they like to refer to one of their creation stories. These stories depict the origins of important realities, practices, and institutions. Some tell how land came to be. Others account for the origins of agriculture, medicines, animal behaviors, the movements of the sun and moon, the songs of birds, the causes of sickness, the foundations of cultural traditions, the names of specific landmarks, and so on. Many Native American creation stories relate the origins of the first human beings. Several of these stories say that the original people emerged from the interior of the earth. The earth, in this type of account, resembles a mother. In her womb, she nurtures the proto-humans. When they are ready, they emerge to the surface to become complete human beings. According to the Hopis' emergence story, before their ancestors left the underworld they were asked to choose how they would live. They elected a hard and humble life raising blue corn. Later, the god Masaw taught the Hopis the right way to plant and care for this crop.

Not all Hopis nurture relationships with Masaw and other Hopi gods, nor do all plant blue corn. Like any other people, Hopis disagree among themselves regarding religious life. They struggle with the challenges of making sense of reality. They work hard to reconcile religious traditions with the postmodern world of computers, corporations, and capitalism. Sometimes they fail, grow frustrated, argue, and divide. Nevertheless, an impressive truth remains: for fifteen hundred years Hopi people have planted blue corn in the same place. It is likely they will continue to do so for many more generations. One of their mesa-top villages, Old Oraibi, contends for the title of the oldest continuously inhabited village in North America. What their ceremonial chiefs and elders declared in 1951 remains true today for many Hopis: "Our land, our religion, and our life are one."

That identical statement could be affirmed by many of the Koyukon people of Alaska, but they would give it different content. Living far to the north where agriculture is impossible, they nevertheless connect their religion with the landscape and their way of life. For them, however, the sacred dimension of life is not explored through digging dirt and planting seeds, but through observing and hunting the animals of central Alaska. Many Koyukon people affirm that animals have spirits. Some of these spirits—living in the brown bear, black bear, wolverine, lynx, wolf, and otter, among other animals—are very powerful.

An elaborate moral code governs how the Koyukon relate to these spirits. The code, in turn, derives from oral tradition, a rich collection of stories set in the Distant Time, the time of beginnings. These stories teach the Koyukon what and who is sacred. Animals figure large in these stories, exercising a powerful influence on creation itself. For example, a story recorded by anthropologist Richard Nelson recalls the influence Raven had on rivers. *Kk' adonts'idnee*, "in the Distant Time it is said," Raven made the rivers so that they flowed both ways, "upstream on one side and downstream on the other. But this made life too easy for humans, he decided, because their boats could drift along in either direction without paddling. So Raven altered his creation and made the rivers flow only one way, which is how they remain today."

Guided by Distant Time stories, the Koyukon people enjoy an intimacy with their surroundings that is difficult for outsiders to comprehend. To be sure, outsiders can learn some of the Koyukon people's stories. They can begin to appreciate the moral code by which the Koyukon live. But without actually living as Koyukons live and living *where* they live, outsiders can never fully understand their religion or convert to it. Koyukon religion, like that of the Hopis, is tied to a way of life, a distinct community, a particular language, and a specific landscape. The link to land distinguishes Koyukon religion from "world religions" such as Christianity, Buddhism, and Islam. Those religions are different, portable; they can be practiced anywhere. Koyukon religion, in contrast, cannot be exported from central Alaska. It belongs there just as surely as Hopi religion belongs in northern Arizona. Koyukon missionaries will never knock on your door. Traditional Hopis will not try to convert you.

Nor will traditional White Mountain Apaches. Like the religions of traditional Hopis and Koyukons, their religion is land-based. It ties White Mountain Apaches to a specific landscape in a profound way. Traditional White Mountain Apaches not only revere the land, they look to it for guidance. Their sacred stories link ethics to the landscape. For White Mountain Apaches, religion means nothing without dirt; morality comes from the earth.

White Mountain Apaches associate thousands of specific sites in east central Arizona with specific traditional stories. These stories relate the powerful actions of gods, the comic antics of cultural heroes like Old Man Owl, the noble struggles of their human ancestors, even the everyday triumphs and failures of contemporary Apache men and women. By telling these stories, Apaches invoke the memory of what took place at specific places. By selecting carefully which stories to tell at a particular instance, Apaches communicate important moral lessons to each other. In so doing, they can teach each other how to lead a good life, a life untainted by jealousy, envy, or arrogance. Among Apaches who know the language, the stories, and the landscape, an amazingly condensed form of communication becomes possible. By merely mentioning a strategically selected place-name, a thoughtful Apache can invoke the right story to communicate a spiritual truth of life-changing power to another Apache. This takes intellectual quickness, knowledge of the storytelling tradition, a good memory, and the courage to take a risk. Apache religion depends upon individual initiative and communal involvement.

For example, one summer during the 1980s, an Apache woman worried about her younger brother's inattention to Apache religion. He had handled a snakeskin, a careless act sure to produce spiritual harm. A friend told her, *"Tséé Hadigaiyé yú 'ágodzaa."* In English, according to anthropologist Keith Basso, this means "it happened at Line of White Rocks Extends Up And Out, at this very place!" A place-name, *Tséé Hadigaiyé yú 'ágodzaa* evokes a specific story associated with that site. The story tells of how an innocent youth behaved irresponsibly, suffered, but ultimately recovered and learned the values of patience and mindfulness. By mentioning the right place-name, the woman reminded her friend of an appropriate story. This gave the worried woman a way to understand what was happening. She could connect her brother's error with a treasured story from her people's tradition, a story tied to the sacred landscape around them. It also comforted the woman to know that her friend cared how she was coping, that her friend had labored to remember a story in the first place, and selected a reassuring one in the second.

Another example illustrates the importance of the landscape among contemporary Apaches, the way physical environment, morality, and religion are fused for many of them. A young woman behaved disrespectfully at a girls' puberty ceremony, wearing pink plastic curlers instead of letting her hair flow free. The next day, at a meal that included the girl and several other people, her grandmother told a story about an Apache man who copied white people too much. Later arrested for rustling, the man came to a bad end. By telling the story, the grandmother sought to "shoot" the young woman, to make her reflect on her ways. Among the Apaches, as among many Native American peoples, women possess spiritual power, and respected elder women exercise important spiritual and social authority. The grandmother's story worked. Each time the young woman passed the place where the man had lived, she thought about her own behavior and determined to lead a good life, an Apache life. Her grandmother's story shamed her, now the landscape reminded her. "I know that place," she admitted to a non-Apache friend. "It stalks me every day." To this young Apache woman, the landscape speaks a powerful moral message. Nick Thompson, an Apache man, concludes: "The land looks after us. The land keeps badness away." To Apaches, the landscape aids moral development and sustains religious life.

Far away, near the Great Lakes, the landscape is very different: wetter, colder, flatter, and more heavily forested than eastern Arizona. But on Fond du Lac Reservation in northern Minnesota, the Anishinaabe people feel as connected to their land as do the White Mountain Apaches to theirs. Anishinaabeg (also known as Ojibwas and Chippewas) do not have easy lives. They contend with unemployment, poverty, discrimination, and other serious problems. Despair, violence, and alcoholism mar many lives and destroy others. But it is not all bleak. Diverse things enliven, distract, entertain, and enrich life "on the rez." Romances spark and burn. Gossip circulates endlessly. Parties go all night. Bingo pays off. Jobs open up. Someone tells a funny story. A woman gives birth. Friends gather and sing. And, during ricing season, Anishinaabeg reconnect with the land around them in the manner of their ancestors. This makes all the difference.

An annual event much anticipated by Anishinaabe men and women, this communal activity involves the harvesting of wild rice. A food rich in protein and possessing a nutty taste, wild rice grows naturally in the shallows of area lakes. Pairs of Anishinaabeg canoe through the stands of ripe rice to gather the heavy grains. Anishinaabeg admire those who harvest quickly and quietly. Anishinaabe writer Jim Northrup evokes the importance of ricing to his people by telling a story about a fictional character named Luke Warmwater. As Luke drives to the lake, "memories of past ricing seasons came to him. His earliest memories were of playing on the shore while his parents were out ricing. He knew the people enjoyed ricing and there were good feelings all around. Years seemed to melt from people. Grandparents moved about with a light step and without their canes. Laughing and loud talking broke out frequently. The cool crisp morning air, the smell of wood smoke, roasting meat, and coffee were all part of these early childhood memories." Luke's partner Dolly poles the canoe as he gathers the grain. "The sound of other ricers swishing through the rice made a nice rhythm. Luke chuckled when he heard the unmistakable sound of a knocker [stick] hitting a canoe instead of the rice. While loosening up his arm and shoulder muscles, he saw the heavy heads hanging at just the right angle for easy knocking. The sound of the rice falling in the canoe made Luke feel good.

"Everywhere he looked, there was good rice. This patch went all the way across the lake. A bald eagle circled above them. He interpreted this as a good sign."

The story continues and describes visits with kin, a meal of fry bread, deer meat, and green tea, and a round of storytelling. Ricing involves all of this. A good way to gather food to eat or sell, ricing enables Anishinaabeg to reconnect with the landscape, to recall their ancestors, and to recharge their own Indianness. For Anishinaabeg, as for many Native nations, the land matters profoundly. Tied to cherished stories, beloved foods, family memories, vital gods, and influential ancestors, the land is sacred.

This conviction, shared by many contemporary Native peoples, goes back thousands of years. All across North America, in every type of ecological setting, Native peoples perfected ways of living good lives in sacred landscapes. Over the course of millennia, American Indians created hundreds of different religions, some gentler towards nature than others. It is impossible to write the history of all of these religions. We can, however, recall some of the most basic and important types from which more recent religions emerged. These basic types include religions associated with the hunter-gatherer way of life, those tied to early agriculture, and those linked to urban settlement. By examining the past, we gain much greater appreciation of the resiliency and dynamism of Native American religions, how they carry the past forward as well as how they leave it behind or transform traditions. Historical study provides a benchmark for evaluating the present. By examining these contrasting types of religious life, we emphasize again the inherent diversity that characterizes Native American religions. Diverse today, they have always varied one from the other. Finally, by retracing the history of Native American religions, we discern major discontinuities and disruptions that have affected Native American religion. Some of these were caused by Native Americans. Others resulted when non-Natives invaded their lands. We begin, then, with the type of Native American religion that predated all others—the religions tied to the hunter-gatherer ways of life.

Hunter-gatherer ways of life taught their participants to be at home in the world, to find their subsistence by hunting game, fishing, and gathering roots, nuts, berries, wild rice, and other foods provided by the landscape. A good person was one who was attuned to the rhythms of nature. A successful band was one led by a wise shaman or spirit-traveler, a man or woman who could divine the weather and the movements of game animals, discern the causes of sickness, and restore the spiritual balances upset by human neglect or malice. Hunter-gatherers organized hunts, sang songs, danced to celebrate the return of spring, and told sacred stories. They loved life, celebrated births, marked the onset of adulthood, and mourned their dead kin. In some places, they buried dogs, ceremonial goods, and tools with their dead. They did not damage the land too much, but in at least one place, the lower Mississippi valley, some hunter-gatherers constructed an impressive building more than five thousand years ago. The building consists of eleven mounds connected by ridges to form an oval structure three football fields wide. Located near present-day Monroe, Louisiana, this structure was built by men and women who gathered each spring to harvest many plants and cook fish, mussels, and game animals. Perhaps constructed for religious or ceremonial purposes, these mounds serve as lasting reminders that hunter-gatherers did not spend all of their time looking for food. They had rich, complex lives and sometimes they did alter the world around them in significant ways. In addition to constructing mounds, they set select fields on fire annually. Burning kept fields free of trees and encouraged the growth of shrubby plants preferred by deer. Hunter-gatherer religions taught men and women to respect the spirits of living things and of the earth, but it did not impose total passivity. These religions promoted dynamic ways of life that proved successful and sustainable for thousands of years, and indeed, in some cases, right up to the present.

About three thousand years ago, however, some Native peoples began relying more on domesticated crops. Native Americans had practiced some forms of agriculture for generations, but now they started cultivating a wider variety of plants producing edible seeds. These included sunflowers, sumpweed, chenopods, knotweed, pigweed, giant ragweed, and maygrass. To store these seeds and the nuts they gathered, American Indians grew gourds to make containers, but they also began using pottery, including storage pots, on a much larger scale.

This increased reliance on domesticated crops along with new storage technologies encouraged a more sedentary life. It was during this phase, which archaeologists have named the "Woodland" period, that men and women in the east first constructed permanent houses.

With this Native-initiated shift toward horticulture and settled life came new religious emphases and practices. Grander funeral practices emerged and ceremonial architecture spread. Woodland peoples constructed thousands of burial mounds, some of immense size. They also built effigy mounds shaped in the form of animals such as snakes and eagles. These mounds served religious purposes, functioning as symbols of spiritual forces revered by Woodland peoples. Guided by the symbolism communicated in their sacred stories, Woodland peoples carefully shaped their houses, situated their burials, planned their villages, and designed their ceremonial spaces.

Woodland Indians built grand buildings more than seventeen hundred years ago in Newark, Ohio. One of these buildings, the Fairgrounds Circle, dwarfs more famous ceremonial buildings. Three stories tall and more than four hundred yards across, this circular structure could contain six copies of Pueblo Bonita, the great Anasazi building located in Chaco Canyon, New Mexico. The Fairgrounds Circle was begun at the time of Christ. Like the great Jewish temple Christ visited in Jerusalem, this building served a religious purpose: it connected people to the sacred. The connection emerged not just because of the ceremonies people performed at this place, but by the very nature of the place itself. Its design was not random or insignificant. Its form communicated profound religious meanings.

At the center of the Fairgrounds Circle, ancient Native American builders located a charnel house or funeral home, a place where the dead were brought and prepared for the afterlife. At its core sat a stone altar. When archaeologists have examined the altar using careful measurements and chemical tests, they have found evidence of cremation. This confirms that the primary purpose of the whole complex was to serve the needs of the dead. This suggests that these ancient people, called the Hopewellians, loved their kin greatly. And to aid deceased kin in their passage from this world to another, they labored long and hard to construct the great complex at Newark. The building, then, may be thought of as a portal, a gateway or a launching pad to the other world.

Moving basketful by basketful of earth for several generations, Hopewellians encircled the charnel house with a protective structure, the great circular wall. This wall separated the central altar and charnel house from the rest of the world. The thick earth wall hid the inner space from the gaze and noise of passersby. Its shape was significant. Among many Native nations, circles are considered perfect forms that protect those within from ghosts and other malign spirits. The Hopewellians who built the Fairgrounds Circle may have shared this belief. Within the outer circle they constructed two others, including one that resembled a moat. This moat served no military purpose. When moats are used to protect sites from humans, they are placed on the outside of walls to slow attackers, not the inside, where they would impede defenders. The location of the Hopewellians' moats at this and other similar sites suggest their purpose was spiritual. In building their circles and moats, the Hopewellians sought to protect their dead from malicious spirits that might retard their happy passage from this world to another. Loving their kin and desiring that the spirits of the dead not linger too long among the living, they labored hard to build the Fairgrounds Circle.

Additional religious symbolism shaped the labor as well. Hopewellians, like most Native Americans, thought about the time of creation with the help of a sacred story. This story told of a hero who dived underwater to retrieve the first earth. That first earth provided the foundations for an entire new world and new forms of life. No copy of the Hopewellian version of this tale exists. Fortunately, other peoples' versions do. According to folklorist George Lankford, the Muskogee people tell it this way: "The time was, in the beginning, when the earth overflowed with water. There was no earth, no beast of the earth, no human being." The Above World beings "held a council to know which would be best, to have some land or to have all water. When the council had met, some said, 'Let us have land, so that we can get food,' because they would starve to death. But others said, 'Let us have all water,' because they wanted it that way.

"So," the Muskogee story continues, "they appointed Eagle as chief. He was told to decide one way or another. Then he decided. He decided for land. So they looked around for some one whom they could send out to get land. The first one to propose himself was Dove, who thought that he could do it. Accordingly they sent him. He was given four days to perform his task. Now, when Dove came back on the fourth day, he said that he could find no land. They concluded to try another plan. Then they obtained the services of Crawfish (*sakdju*). He went down through the water into the ground beneath, and he too was gone four days. On the fourth morning he arose and appeared on the surface of the waters. In his claws they saw that he held some dirt. He had at last secured the land. Then they took the earth from his claws and made a ball of it. When this was completed they handed it over to the chief, Eagle, who took it and went out from their presence with it. When he came back to the council, he told them that there was land, an island. So all the beasts went in the direction pointed out, and found that there was land there as Eagle had said. But what they found was very small. They lived there until the water receded from this earth. Then the land all joined into one."

This version of the story belongs to the Muskogee nation. Also known as the Creek people, the Muskogee nation originally lived in the southeast, in Alabama and Georgia. Forcibly removed by the United States during the 1830s, most of them live now in the heart of the continent, in Oklahoma. That is where this story was recorded in 1904. But Muskogee storytellers and poets have told the story for centuries. They have celebrated the deeds of Crawfish and Eagle for countless generations.

Several Native peoples tell a creation story similar to that of the Muskogees. Cherokee, Delaware, Omaha, Seneca, Kansa, Shawnee, Hopi, Navajo, Acoma, Yakima, and other peoples tell or used to tell a story focused on a deep-diving animal hero. In the Cherokee version, the Earth-Diver is a water beetle. According to Anishinaabeg, Ottawas, Mesquakies, and Onondagas, it was a muskrat. For Arikaras it was a duck, for Cheyennes a mudhen, for Arapahos a red-headed duck and a turtle, and so on. Told across great stretches of America among dozens of Native nations, the Earth-Diver story is probably among the most widespread of all Native American creation stories, and one of the oldest.

Because Hopewellians revered the Earth-Diver story, they associated the beginning of life on earth with the hero who dives underwater and returns to the surface with a bit of dirt. This creation story influenced their beliefs concerning the afterlife, their burial rituals, and their mortuary architecture. For Hopewellians mud had symbolic power, a power they sought to tap in behalf of their dead. Hopewellians used a special kind of mud to cover burials and charnel houses. Coating these structures with puddled clay, a mixture of water and dirt from the bottom of a streambed, they protected their dead from chaos and brought them closer to the powers of creation. At Fairgrounds Circle, Hopewellians made an even bolder connection to the sacred story of Earth-Diver. They had noted that when something enters or leaves the middle of a pond—for example, a duck—it produces a circular wave that spreads and rolls across the surface of the water.

Having witnessed this phenomenon and associating it with the Earth-Diver's epic emergence from the waters, they attempted to represent it architecturally: they built a great circular moat and wall around a central "emergence" point. The dirt wall was like a wave receding from the center point. The purpose of this structure seems clear. Placing their dead at the center, Hopewellians hoped to enable their loved ones to "emerge" from this world and go into the next. The structure gave concrete form to the sacred story. By entering the structure, Hopewellians gained better access to the powers of creation. There could be no better point to begin the next phase of one's spiritual journey.

Roger G. Kennedy, former director of the National Park Service, has studied this place carefully. He imagines visitors heard special music and encountered special smells as they approached the great circle. "Some had passed through the confined space of the Great Hopewell road, accompanied by flutes and drums and incantations for fifty miles." In special sheltered areas off of the main road, Hopewellians prepared themselves by smoking strong tobacco in pipes decorated with the images of birds. The tobacco cleared the mind and produced smoke rising to the heavens. Birds, because they move between earth and sky, symbolized the movement from flesh to spirit, from life to death, from this world to the next. Only after these preparations were Hopewellians ready to enter the great circle. There they prepared the dead for burial, but also for rebirth. In the graves of loved ones, Hopewellians placed small sculptures of birds, one more sign that they associated death with a transition, not a termination.

The Hopewellians were neither the first nor the last American Indians to construct sacred earth-works on a monumental scale. Along the lower Mississippi, at a place called Poverty Point in Louisiana, more than three thousand years ago a thriving civilization built a complex of concentric half circles. These circles included an outermost ring measuring four-fifths of a mile across and focused on a mound two hundred yards square and four stories tall. From this Gulf Coast center radiated a trade network that extended to the Atlantic Ocean in the east, the Great Lakes in the north, and the Rocky Mountains in the west. Along this network, travelers carried small quantities of rare materials useful in sacred art: hematite, galena, quartz, copper, sharks' teeth, and shells. Less traders than pilgrims, they may have traveled great distances to reach the ceremonial center in Louisiana.

Thriving at the time when the Israelites were escaping Egyptian bondage and the ancient Greek poet Homer was singing of his people's gods, this civilization and its religion remain largely unknown or unappreciated by modern Americans. Archaeologists uncover jasper sculptures of clams, falcons, and owls, but they cannot retrieve this culture's epics, prayers, chants, creation stories, psalms, mythologies, liturgies, manners, ethics, and songs. Without access to this oral tradition, we cannot understand fully their religion and how it inspired them to fashion these great earth-works. The architecture of this civilization remains visible and impressive, but the reasons for its rise and eventual fall elude us.

Much better known is the story of the last moundbuilders, the Native Americans known as the Mississippians because of their links to the great river. Their civilization emerged a thousand years ago in the southeast, spread up the Mississippi valley, reached into Illinois and Missouri, and affected the Great Lakes region as well. This civilization was based on intensive production of a new type of corn. With the surpluses provided by this new crop came needs for large-scale food storage and protection of dispersed farmsteads. The solution came in the form of a fortified center where goods could be stored and distributed. In part, this development was pragmatic. In part, it was religious, for Mississippians linked their distribution centers to the burial mounds. Burial mounds had long served as powerful embodiments of basic religious ideas. Their form gave tangible substance to abstract principles and beliefs. Mounds reminded people of stories of creation. They served as ceremonial centers. People gathered nearby to trade. The Mississippians added additional functions. The mortuary mound became the administrative, physical, and religious center of Mississippian society.

Woodland Indians had built circular mounds; Mississippians built square, flat-topped ones. Periodically, Mississippians would add a new blanket of earth to the mound, symbolically burying it and restoring its purity. Its purity was important, for the mound was the center, the place where the most important rites of the Mississippians were performed. The mound functioned as a sacred platform, a place where earth met sky. Yet, if all Mississippian town-dwellers participated in constructing and renewing their mounds, not all had equal access to it. Unlike previous mound-building civilizations, this one was hierarchical, meaning that some individuals had greater privileges and powers than others.

Access to the top of the mound was limited to an elite class of chiefs and priests. The chiefs controlled esoteric knowledge related to warfare and mythological beings such as the great winged snake. In life and death, the chiefs' clans wore, possessed, and manipulated specially crafted objects of rare materials that symbolized their influence in warfare. These objects included engraved shell cups and stone axes. To supply these and other rare goods, an extensive trade network evolved, connecting Mississippians to each other and to peoples and regions far away.

As for the priests, they cared for the memory of illustrious ancestors and managed rituals performed in permanent mound-top temples. The Mississippian temple featured stone, wood, and ceramic statuary of human figures, often depicting birth or death. Priests enjoyed access to the temple mound and were thought to have the power to influence the forces of life and death. Mississippian priests played a vital social role. They helped weld the elite warrior class together with the more common folk who produced all of the food. They did this by calling attention to overarching shared symbols that unified all members of the society. This society relished symbols of the sun, the source of heat, light, and the power to make things grow. Priests acted as expert observers of the daily, seasonal, and annual cycles of the sun.

Priests also supervised rituals that brought everyone into concert. Corn was sacred for Mississippians, agriculture a holy labor bringing human beings into a profound, sacramental relationship with the powers that made life possible. Mississippians did not dig the earth casually, but thankfully. They said prayers when they planted seeds. They lit new fires and sacrificed sacred foods when they gathered the first harvest of the year. Priests oversaw these activities, ensuring that people respected basic taboos, planted at the right time, and did not harvest prematurely. They supervised ceremonies linked to the life cycle of corn and sought the blessings of spirits governing rain. In this corn-based, sun-centered civilization, priests were centrally important. They belonged on the mound.

In spite of the best efforts of priests to promote order and fertility, Mississippian societies were not stable. A community might build mounds for a few generations, then stop suddenly. Centers of construction shifted across the landscape with no clear pattern. However, some lasted long enough to attract large concentrations of people. Cahokia, located near modern St. Louis, involved more than ten thousand people. It was the greatest American town for centuries. Near the Mississippi River, the residents of Cahokia constructed a pyramid that rivaled those in Egypt. Then, in the fourteenth century, Cahokia faded in importance.

Around the same time, something similar seems to have occurred in a very different landscape far to the west of the Mississippi valley. In the Dolores and San Juan valleys of Colorado and New Mexico, an impressive civilization involved thirty thousand people. Like Mississippians, Anasazi men and women grew corn, prayed for rain, and closely observed the movements of the stars, moon, and sun. Unlike Mississippians, they built permanent stone villages and storage buildings in spectacular cliff settings. They also constructed special subterranean spaces called kivas to have a place to meet, perform ceremonies, and discuss religious issues. These structures, along with their impressive villages, survive today in excellent condition. They draw tens of thousands of tourists annually to places like Mesa Verde, Colorado. Tourists gaze into dark and empty kivas and try to imagine the lives of the people who once worshiped there.

What some tourists tend to forget, however, is that the Anasazis did not disappear. If their kivas are empty, it is because the Anasazis of Mesa Verde abandoned them long ago. They moved southward into New Mexico. Perhaps drought pushed them out of their home; maybe a new religious movement pulled them to a new one. Regardless, the people changed and survived. Among their descendants are modern Pueblo Indians of New Mexico and Arizona. Today descendants of Anasazis attend college, drive trucks, work in mines, staff casinos, make art, and do all the other things contemporary Americans do. Sometimes considered among the most traditional of all American Indians, the Pueblo Indians carry forward into the twenty-first century some beliefs and spiritual values thousands of years old.

The Anasazi culture was never an urban one where people concentrated in dense cities. Its participants lived in dispersed homesteads and small villages. This contrasted with the situation in Mexico. At the time of Columbus, there flourished in Mexico an unmistakably urban civilization, a real empire. Involving hundreds of thousands if not millions of people, the Aztec empire centered on a great city, Tenochtitlán. Its 250,000 residents made it perhaps the largest city in the world at the end of the fifteenth century.

Aztecs considered their city a sacred place. They said a god had selected its location—an island in a lake in central Mexico—expressly for their ancestors, the Mexica people. On this promised land, the Aztecs constructed a lively city with permanent buildings dedicated to military, religious, commercial, artistic, and educational purposes. Everything focused on a ceremonial center that included twenty-five major pyramids. A civilized people, the Aztecs cultivated a high regard for beauty, manners, and order. And they performed rituals involving human sacrifice. Indeed, Aztecs slaughtered thousands of captives and many of their own people. Historian Inga Clendinnen provides a graphic portrait of their bloody ceremonies. As she reports, these took place "not only in the main temple precinct, but in the neighborhood temples and on the streets. On high occasions warriors carrying gourds of human blood or wearing the dripping skins of their captives ran through the streets, to be ceremoniously welcomed into the dwellings; the flesh of their victims seethed in domestic cooking pots; human thighbones, scraped and dried, were set up in the courtyards of the households." What may seem bizarre to us made sense to them. The sacred forces of their world were capricious. Civilization depended upon spectacular rites of sacrifice. Human blood supplied the most worthy offering.

The city of Tenochtitlán awed all who saw it. A Spaniard named Bernal Díaz, who visited it in 1519, recorded his fellow soldiers' initial reaction: "When we saw all those cities and villages built in the water, and other great towns on dry land, and that straight and level causeway leading to Mexico, we were astounded. . . . The great towns and pyramids and buildings rising from the water, all made of stone, seemed like an enchanted vision from the tale of Amadis. Indeed, some of our soldiers asked whether it was not all a dream." Another said, "In Spain there is nothing to compare with it." Others thought it grander than Constantinople and Rome. The city's impressive scale and architecture, however, did not intimidate the Spanish or persuade them to spare it. Led by Hernando Cortés and allied with the Aztecs' enemies, they waged war, lost battles, won battles, and finally conquered the city. In 1520, the Spanish leveled the city and began replacing Aztec buildings with their own. Stones from Aztec temples provided the foundations for Catholic churches.

The Spanish prevailed in part because a terrible disease killed many Aztec men, women, and children. According to an Aztec account, smallpox "spread over the people with great destruction of men." This disease did not seriously affect the Spanish. The Spanish carried it, but did not suffer its worst effects. European and African ancestors of the Spanish had been exposed to the disease for many generations. Over time, the Spanish had developed immunity to it. Because the Aztecs' ancestors had never encountered the disease, the Aztecs inherited no immunity whatsoever. The Aztecs, like all Native American peoples, were radically vulnerable to smallpox and other European diseases. They died in staggering numbers.

What happened in Mexico was repeated elsewhere. Throughout the Americas, smallpox and other diseases introduced by Europeans—chicken pox, influenza, measles, mumps, typhus, cholera, whooping cough, and others—killed millions of men, women, and children. It is impossible to fathom the suffering, let alone quantify the numbers who died. Because scholars cannot determine how many people lived in the Americas before these epidemics, we cannot determine their full impact. Estimates for the pre-Columbian population of the United States and Canada range wildly, from a low of 3.8 million to a high of 12.2 million. Everyone agrees many more people lived in Mexico and Central America, perhaps 30 million, with an additional 10 million residing in South America.

Whatever the precise number for any given region, it is clear that a great proportion died. Almost all nations suffered. Contagious microbes did not discriminate among Hopi and Pueblo farmers, Koyukon hunter-gatherers, Mississippian villagers, and Aztec city dwellers. None of these people possessed the necessary immunities. Just as weeds thrive in unused soil, so diseases flourished in America. At some point or other, outbreaks struck Native nations in Arizona and Alaska, Minnesota and Mexico, not to mention Newfoundland and Florida, California and Carolina, and every place in between. Coastal peoples and island-dwellers suffered first and most intensely, but American Indians who lived in concentrated settlements were also more likely to be exposed. In some places, 90 percent of a nation died from diseases. All in all, this was the worst natural holocaust ever experienced in human history, the most terrible tragedy in the Americas.

Somehow, miraculously, incredibly, Native America survived the catastrophe caused by the outsiders. If diseases killed millions, it did not wipe out Native American nations altogether. Native people became much less visible in the areas where Europeans first settled, but they regained strength in the interior regions. Far to the interior, some Indian peoples lived beyond direct European influence, north of the reach of the Spanish, west or south of the reach of the English and French. Everywhere American Indians began the long process of adapting to life in the new world created by unprecedented diseases and the novel presence of diverse European and African peoples in the Americas. They succeeded.

In part, they succeeded because of their religious creativity and spiritual resiliency. The massive epidemics hurt Native American religions and introduced major disruptions, but did not destroy them. A shaman died, but a hunter remembered the songs of his father. A priest perished, but a seed-planter remembered the chants of her mother. People stopped building mounds, but parents continued to tell their children the stories of creation, how the Earth-Diver dived to find the first earth, and where the first people emerged from their mother. Disease struck without mercy, but grandmothers continued to evoke the memory of what happened at particular places to instruct young people in good behavior. Everywhere, the animals continued to carry spiritual power. Nowhere did the sun fail to rise and provide a reassuring sense of regularity. Always, the moon pursued her cycles with constancy. People died, but the people did not stop living, watching, and debating how to be good human beings in this complex world.

The Navajo creation story describes the formation of key things deemed important in Navajo religion. A previous section describes the origins of First Man and First Woman in an underworld called the "First World." When this world becomes filled with strife, they leave and, along with two supernatural companions, journey through additional underworlds. In the "Third World," they witness the creation of six mountains, the misty precursors of those revered by contemporary Navajos. This version of the story was related in 1928 by Sandoval, translated by Sam Ahkeah, and recorded by Aileen O'Bryan.

The bluebird was the first to reach the Third or Yellow World. After him came the First Four and all the others.

A great river crossed this land from north to south. It was the Female River. There was another river crossing it from east to west, it was the Male River. The Male River flowed through the Female River and on; and the name of this place is Tóbil dahask'id, Where the Streams Come Together.

There were six mountains in the Third World. In the East was Sisnaajiní [Mt. Baldy near Alamosa, Colorado], the Standing Black Sash. Its ceremonial name is the Dawn or White Shell Mountain. In the South stood Tsoodzil, the Great Mountain, also called Mountain Tongue [Mt. Taylor, near Grants, New Mexico]. Its ceremonial name is the Blue Bead or Turquoise Mountain. In the West stood Dook'o'slííd [San Francisco Peak, in Flagstaff, Arizona], and the meaning of this name is forgotten. Its ceremonial name is the Abalone Shell Mountain. In the North Dib'nitsaa [San Juan Mountains in Colorado], Many Sheep Mountain. Its ceremonial name is Obsidian Mountain. Then there was Dzil ná'oodilii [El Huerfano Peak, New Mexico], the Upper Mountain. It was very sacred; and its name means also the Center Place, and the people moved around it. Its ceremonial name is Precious Stone or Banded Rock Mountain. There was still another mountain called Ch'óol'jj [also El Huerfano or El Huerfanito Peak, New Mexico], or Giant Spruce Mountain, and it was also a sacred mountain.

There was no sun in this land, only the two rivers and the six mountains.

CHAPTER TWO

Traditions and Crisis in the Eastern Woodlands

More than two hundred years ago, a European named John Heckewelder witnessed a dramatic event in an Ohio forest involving a Native American hunter and a bear. As Heckewelder later wrote, the hunter, a member of the Delaware Indian nation, shot the bear and the musket ball "broke its backbone. The animal fell and set up a most plaintive cry, something like that of the cougar when he is hungry. The hunter, instead of giving him another shot, stood up close to him, and addressed him in these words: 'Hark ye! bear; you are a coward, and no warrior as you pretend to be. Were you a warrior, you would show it by your firmness and not cry and whimper like an old woman. You know, bear, that our tribes are at war with each other, and that yours was the aggressor. You have found the Indians too powerful for you, and you have gone sneaking about in the woods, stealing their hogs; perhaps at this time you have hog's flesh in your belly. Had you conquered me, I would have borne it with courage and died like a brave warrior; but you, bear, sit here and cry, and disgrace your tribe by your cowardly conduct.'"

The hunter's behavior puzzled Heckewelder, a Moravian missionary of German ancestry. The German, English, Swedish, and Dutch colonists he knew did not talk to animals, let alone berate them. Heckewelder asked the Delaware Indian man "how he thought the poor animal could understand what he said to it." The hunter answered confidently, "The bear understood me well; did you not observe how ashamed he looked while I was upbraiding him?" Heckewelder, unconvinced, concluded that the Delaware people held "strange notions."

The hunter's behavior, however, was in no way strange or unusual when viewed from the perspective of his fellow Delaware Indians. The reason was simple. During the eighteenth century, many Delaware Indians considered natural phenomena—animals, plants, stones, rivers—to be "persons." These phenomena, although not human, possessed spiritual power and had a social identity. They all deserved respect. Bears especially warranted careful attention.

Physically dangerous but also intelligent, bears resembled humans in their capacity to stand upright, in their ability to emit cries of pain, and in many other ways. Their hunting skills inspired fear and admiration. Bears, unlike other animals, could switch roles with the human hunters who pursued them. They could turn human hunters into the hunted, hopeful predators into unwilling prey. Hunting and killing a bear was like stalking and killing an enemy warrior. All across North America, Native Americans regarded bears with great respect. For many peoples, bears held great spiritual significance.

Bear hunting required careful preparation. Before beginning a hunt, Native American men scrutinized their dreams and relied upon other forms of divination, looking for signs that would tell when and where to hunt. They also observed special behavioral taboos. Male hunters among the Shawnee, Creek, Cherokee, Cree, and many other Native American peoples avoided contact with menstruating women. These hunters assumed menstrual blood, associated with the positive forces of life, would overwhelm their power to kill. Merely walking near a menstruating woman or swimming downstream from where she had bathed would ruin a hunter's magic.

In order to protect the power of hunters, some Native American peoples sequestered menstruating women until their periods passed. During their menses, Creek and Cherokee women, for example, stayed in isolated huts away from their villages. This practice acknowledged the extraordinary power adult women possessed. It also provided them with a regular, sanctioned break from their regular activities of tending crops, processing game, gathering wild foods, making pottery and baskets, counseling elders, consoling friends, romancing lovers. While a woman rested in the hut, her children were taken care of by a large extended family, including her sisters, brothers, and parents. Childrearing, after all, was not the exclusive duty of biological mothers. The duty was shared by a wider circle of people. To raise a Native American child, it took not just a loving mother; it took a vibrant clan and a stable community.

Upon leaving the safety of the village clearing, hunters entered the more dangerous realm of the forest and focused on the drama of the hunt itself. They told each other stories of past hunts. They sang special songs to gather power. They prepared special bundles of symbolic objects to aid their efforts. They concentrated on their prey.

Individual hunters in the field sang special songs, seductive songs designed to relax the animals and draw them near. When hunting bears in the Appalachian mountains, some Cherokee hunters sang the following song:

> In Rabbit Place you were conceived Yoho!
> In Mulberry Place you were conceived Yoho!
> In Uyaye you were conceived—Yoho!
> In the Great Swamp you were conceived—Yoho!

By approaching animals in the proper way, a hunter was supposed to have greater success finding and shooting prey.

Hunting required practical skill, but it also involved a spiritual exchange of a highly charged sort. After shooting an animal, a hunter tried to convince the creature's spirit that he had acted in a morally justifiable manner. Two major strategies existed. A hunter might apologize to the victim, lamenting the necessity that made humans kill for meat, asserting his own innocence and sorrow. Or a hunter might try to shift blame to the victim, asserting that it belonged to an enemy "tribe." Either way, hunters sought to avoid alienating the spirit of the animal. An alienated spirit would carry news of the insult to its kind and then those animals would cease to allow the hunter and his people to take them. Or, the alienated species might exact some form of vengeance, sending sickness to hunters or killing the hunters' kin.

The Delaware hunter knew exactly what he was doing when he yelled at the bear. Treating the animal as if bears were sworn "enemies" of humans, the victorious hunter cajoled his ursine victim, reminding him of the "war" between humans and bears. The Delaware hunter hoped his words would convince the spiritually potent animal not to hold a grudge. But he may also have been talking to himself. Aware of the similarity between bears and humans and perhaps disturbed by the extraordinary suffering of an animal shot in the spine, he may have felt guilty. Not desiring to feel like a murderer, he sought to rationalize his violence.

Many Native Americans thought it important to treat an animal's carcass with care. They thought that if they mistreated an animal's body and alienated its spirit, disease would strike. Eastern Woodland Native Americans related many ailments to animals; for example, they named various maladies "deer eyes" disease, "tongue of deer" disease, and "deer chief" disease. As a Cherokee story concluded, "No hunter who has regard for his health ever fails to ask pardon of the Deer for killing it."

Similarly, a Delaware Indian story related the grotesque consequences that awaited hunters who behaved badly and disregarded the feelings of living animals. In the story, a boy named A-sun-Ke-pon, "Rock-Shut-Up," abuses bears by wounding them, then letting them go. In revenge, the bears play a mean trick on him, messing with his mind and body. They ambush him, rip his arms and legs off, put them back on, and then release him. As soon as he reaches home, however, his limbs fall off. The moral was clear. Human beings who abused game animals would suffer serious consequences. This was a lesson Delaware boys needed to learn. The story taught it as effectively as any book of moral philosophy or learned sermon.

Different peoples had different rules governing butchering procedures and disposal of animals. Although men usually did most of the hunting, women helped process the meat. Young women accompanied their mates to hunting camps. They cleaned the game, tanned the hides, and cooked the food. In these ways, they helped take something wild and transform it into something socially useful.

Before consuming game, many Native American hunters offered a piece of meat to the campfire, feeding the spirits they thought had helped them have success. Creek Indians revered the fire itself. Among the Delawares, some hunters sacrificed meat to owls; these super-alert birds were said to bring success to hunters. After making these sacrifices, hunters ate, completing a ritual cycle that had begun in prayer and song.

Just as many Native Americans thought animals possessed spirits, many also believed the same of plants. Plants, wild and domestic, were essential to the diet of Native American peoples across North America. In the east, corn ruled. Grown primarily by women, maize satisfied far more of the caloric needs of eastern peoples than did hunting or fishing. Although they were expert farmers, many colonial Native Americans did not take corn or any other traditional crop for granted. Rather they viewed plants such as beans, squash, and corn as gifts from sacred beings. They celebrated these and other plants in religious ceremonies.

Delawares staged a twelve-day harvest ceremony in the fall. This ceremony, marking their New Year, took place in a large, bark-shingled, log-walled structure. The building had an eastern opening to point toward the direction of birth and a western opening that pointed toward death. Inside, twelve masks were carved into eleven posts supporting the roof. For Delawares, the number twelve signified the number of levels of the cosmos. Each post had one mask, except for the central one, which featured two. These central masks represented the Creator, the life force that supported everything else. To the east and west sides of this central post, a fire burned. An oval path circled these fires. Dancers moved along the path in a way that represented the spirit's journey after earthly life.

Delawares were not the only people who choreographed sacred dances. Among many peoples throughout North America, dance and worship went together. Some Shawnees performed the Bread Dance in the spring to guarantee a good harvest in warmer seasons. Many Cherokees staged the Green Corn Dance to thank the Creator and the Corn Mother for their summer crops. Most Creeks performed this and other dances. William Bartram, an eighteenth-century traveler in Creek country, said they knew "an endless variety of [dance] steps." Many were associated with animals. The snow, fox, and snake dances were performed only by women. In the mosquito dance, women pricked male dancers with pins. Other dances performed by the Creeks included the horse dance, chicken dance, buffalo dance, duck dance, small frog dance, screech owl dance, horned owl dance, beaver dance, quail dance, crane dance, bean dance, and buzzard dance. Not every one of these was a religious dance, but each in some way encouraged Creeks to think more deeply about their relationship with the nonhuman persons living in their homeland.

Creeks also staged an elaborate ceremony celebrating corn. Corn was their mainstay, as it had been for their Mississippian ancestors. Residing in the moist, sunny southeast, Creeks often grew two crops of corn in one season. In some Creek towns, the ceremony, usually occurring in late summer, lasted eight days and nights, and involved a wholesale cleansing of the village, the repair of the ceremonial buildings that defined the "square ground," and special rites focused on renewing the town's sacred fire.

An eighteenth-century English traveler who witnessed the Creek Green Corn ceremony in the town of Little Tallassie recalled how a Creek religious leader, "dressed in white leather moccasins and stockings," created "the new fire, which he accomplishes with much labor by the friction of two sticks. After the fire is produced, four young men enter the openings at the four corners of the square, each having a stick of wood for the new fire; they approach the fire with much reverence." They placed "the ends of the wood" they carried "in a very formal manner" so that the sticks pointed "to the four cardinal points." This invoked the entirety of creation. It was appropriate. The Green Corn Ceremony, Creeks believed, renewed the whole world. The old year ended and a new one began. Crimes other than murder were forgiven.

Once ignited, the new fire was fed with sacrifices of new corn, portions of bear oil, fresh deer meat, button snake-root medicine, and yaupon tea leaves, the source of an important ceremonial beverage consumed at daybreak by Creek men. In this way, Creeks celebrated the things that the Maker of Breath, their great god, had put in their land so that they could have a good life.

Through a great variety of ceremonies, songs, and dances, Native Americans expressed their sense that life was a deeply spiritual affair. "On the approach of a storm or thunder-gust," Delaware Indians, according to John Heckewelder, prayed to the god of the air. "I have also seen the Chippeways, on the Lakes of the Canada, pray to the Mannitto [spirit power] of the waters, that he might prevent the swells from rising too high, while they were passing over them." In both cases, reverent Native Americans sacrificed tobacco in gratitude. Mohawk travelers did something similar when crossing Lake George in upstate New York. They placed specially prepared bundles of tobacco on the particular rock where the god of the wind resided. Once, however, in 1667, Mohawk travelers performing the ceremony were interrupted by a rude Dutch man. According to a historian's account written in 1727, Arlent van Curler scoffed at the Mohawks' ceremony and "turn'd up his Back-side towards the Rock." Swift consequences followed. The wind turned ferocious, capsizing his boat, and Van Curler drowned.

Not every American Indian, let alone each and every Mohawk, connected the wind to a spirit. Native Americans disagreed on many things. Speaking hundreds of different languages and thousands of dialects, or regional variations, their cultural and religious diversity cannot be overestimated. No generalization characterizes all Native Americans. However, during the colonial period, it seems clear that for many Native American men and women in the eastern woodlands and elsewhere, life involved an ever-shifting flow of charged exchanges between and among human and nonhuman persons. Many Native Americans felt that hunting, planting, harvesting, gathering, fishing, canoeing, and other actions shifted the balances. Many of them thought they could try to restore the preferred balances through speeches, symbolic acts, ritual sacrifices, special songs, and strategic gestures. They also sensed that they never could achieve perfect or permanent equilibrium. For people who felt like this, the spiritual drama never stopped. In the night, meteors streaked, the wind died down, dogs woofed at shadowy shapes, an owl cried out. The wise person paid attention; the insensitive, slackard, or childish did not.

The Delawares, like other Native American peoples, did not write down their values or the stories that communicated them. Instead, they cultivated the art of storytelling. They gave stories an important place in their lives. Nora Thompson Dean, a Unami Delaware traditionalist, stressed this point: "Long, long time ago there were professional storytellers . . . The storyteller carried a bag, and when he'd tell a story, then he'd remove some of these little rocks, or beads, or seeds, cornseeds, and he'd set those to one side. And after he took care of all these grains, he was exhausted then, the stories was all over." For their efforts, storytellers received food, hospitality, and respect.

Storytellers expected alert audiences. "You just had to absorb what was told to you," Dean said, describing her own childhood experience of paying attention to her storytelling mother. Children were not supposed to interrupt. Usually they did not want to. Far from boring the young, the Delawares' stories entertained them and their elders, bringing joy to a long winter night, filling the empty time when work ceased or the heavens rained.

In villages and towns across the eastern woodlands, adults used stories to educate the next generation in how to relate to their world. American Indians in New England, for example, told a story concerning the proper treatment of fish. According to the story, a mischievous god had once tricked all the fish in the ocean that the world was coming to an end. This trickster god convinced the fish that only his own river would remain. When all the fish swam up his river into his fish traps, the trickster god took them to his grandmother so that she would no longer have a difficult time obtaining food. But she was very displeased: "Grandson, you have not done well. All the fish will be annihilated. So what will our descendants in the future do to live?" Whereupon the trickster opened the basket and released the surplus fish. The message was clear: if you care about the future, do not be greedy with nature.

While most adults were involved in the moral education of children, in practice women of all ages, especially grandmothers, and elderly men exercised the most influence, because they did not leave the village for long periods of time. They preferred indirect, noncoercive means of instruction. Delawares, for example, taught their traditional morality by praising children who performed good deeds and lamenting those who did bad ones. Heckewelder recorded how this worked:

> If a child is seen passing through the streets leading an old decrepit person, the villagers will in his hearing, and to encourage all the other children who may be present to take example from him, call on one another to look on and see what a *good* child that must be . . . On the other hand, when a child has committed a *bad* act, the parent will say to him: 'O! how grieved I am that my child has done this *bad* act! I hope he will never do so again.'

This method, employed by elders and "seconded by the whole community," produced children who demonstrated a "strong attachment to ancient customs, respect for age, and the love of virtue."

These comments, complaints, and compliments, along with stories, songs, poems, prayers, chants, jokes, place-names, and other forms of speech common among the Delaware people, constituted the Delawares' distinctive oral tradition. More than almost anything else, the oral tradition defined what it meant to be a Delaware Indian. Less based on blood than knowledge of the land and immersion in the language and oral tradition of the people, being Delaware was something that took years to achieve. Remarkably, some white people made the transition. Taken captive in their youth in colonial wars and adopted by Delaware families, they found Delaware life so fulfilling they were reluctant to leave it, even when the opportunity presented itself. Similarly, in 1763, white captives among the Shawnees cried when the English "liberated" them.

From Massachusetts to Georgia, a small number of Europeans and Africans actually ran away to live among Native American peoples. They desired to escape mistreatment or slavery. Others, living as traders married to Native American women, gradually learned how to view the world through Native American eyes. James Adair, an eighteenth-century trader, knew "white people . . . who have become Indian proselytes of justice, by living according to the Indian religious system." These people Adair labeled "white Indians."

The vast majority of European colonists did not adopt Native American religious systems, but this does not mean they were not influenced by Native Americans. Those colonists in closest contact with Native American peoples wore their clothing, employed their diplomatic practices, paddled their canoes, and learned their verbal expressions. Most colonists planted Native American foods. New World crops altered the lives of Europeans who never migrated to America. Potatoes became a mainstay in Poland, Russia, Ireland, and elsewhere in Northern Europe. Tomatoes added color to Italian cuisine. Corn, squash, beans, pumpkins, and many other foods enhanced Europeans' diets and lives. These Native American contributions and others decisively changed European history.

Contact altered the lives of Native Americans just as fundamentally. Diseases, brought by increased contact with Europeans, had devastated the Aztecs in the sixteenth century; epidemics of typhoid, smallpox, influenza, and other illnesses continued to sweep across North America in subsequent centuries. American Indians in New England were hit hard in 1616 and again in 1633. Smallpox killed half of the Cherokees in 1738, then struck Plains Indians and others in 1779. Whenever European diseases reached Native American people who lacked the appropriate immunities, death resulted. Widespread death challenged Native American religions.

During the seventeenth century, devastating epidemics of smallpox caused a social and spiritual crisis among the Iroquois people in the northeast region of upstate New York. The Iroquois consisted of five nations united in a Great League of Peace and Power. Their union had been achieved in the fifteenth century in large part due to the guidance of a religious leader whom the Iroquois call the Peacemaker. The Peacemaker appeared at a time when rampant warfare brought great grief and suffering. He taught thirteen laws that enabled Mohawks, Oneidas, Onondagas, Cayugas, and Senecas to live together in harmony and peace. They called themselves the Hodenosaunee, "the people of the longhouse." The name symbolized their desire to retain a sense of separateness even as they united. The longhouse was the standard Iroquois home. Built of curved saplings covered with sheets of bark, a longhouse could extend more than a hundred feet in length. A single home housed several families. Each family occupied a specific section along the side of the open interior. Each shared a fire with the family across from it. Similarly, each of the five nations of the Hodenosaunee retained its own identity even as it united with the others on the basis of the Peacemaker's teachings.

The league produced peace among its members, but it did not stop the Iroquois from waging war against their other enemies. Before the arrival of Europeans, these wars were chiefly fought for spiritual reasons, not for the purpose of acquiring territory. When a loved one died, Iroquois families mourned deeply and relied upon dramatic rituals to help them deal with their grief. One of these ceremonies, the "requickening," involved the transfer of the deceased person's name and social role to a new person. The need for substitutes for the dead led the Iroquois to engage in "mourning wars." These consisted of small-scale raids on enemies that were designed to bring home captives.

The fate of these captives rested with matriarchs, female elders who exercised significant power in Iroquois society. They might decide the captives should be adopted. Or, they might determine that the captives should be tortured, killed, butchered, and cooked for ritual consumption by the villagers. Adoption enabled Iroquois families to restore their strength. Torture and ritual cannibalism allowed grieving Iroquois to vent their rage against enemies and assimilate the *orenda,* or spiritual power, of captives.

As a result of contact with Europeans, however, this traditional pattern became dysfunctional and counterproductive. After contact intensified in the early seventeenth century, epidemics caused deaths on a scale never before experienced. The need for captives soared, and with it, the incentive for warfare deepened. But, because of trade with Europeans, the modes and consequences of warfare also changed. European firearms made Native American warfare far more dangerous and deadly. To obtain a military advantage over their enemies, the Iroquois sought greater control over the fur trade. The more beaver they harvested, the more firearms they could obtain. Their ancestors had fought small-scale "mourning wars"; seventeenth-century Iroquois began fighting imperial "beaver wars."

The well-armed Iroquois nearly wiped out the Huron people and they subjugated others as well. No nation could match the power of the Iroquois, but the Iroquois paid a heavy price for dominance. Increasingly, their lives became chaotic, dominated by killing and dying. By 1701, the Iroquois determined modern warfare was too costly. In a grand meeting in Montreal, they agreed to confine their hunting to certain areas and to let the French governor of New France settle their conflicts with other nations. This proved a wise move. The Iroquois population increased and their confederacy of five (eventually six) nations remained one of the strongest political forces in the eastern woodlands. During the first half of the eighteenth century, the Iroquois enjoyed a lively trade with the French and the English while avoiding being dominated by them.

Iroquois, along with Algonquins, Anishinaabeg, Delawares, and other northern Native American peoples, traded beaver pelts and other items with Europeans. In exchange, they received guns and ammunition, cloth of all types, rum, mirrors, body paints, tools, tobacco, glass beads, wire, ceramic items, glass bottles, clay pipes, and much more. Meanwhile, in the south, the desire for these same goods led Catawbas,

Cherokees, Choctaws, Creeks, and Seminoles to hunt deer and process deerskins as never before. Trade connected Native American peoples to the larger Atlantic world that included the citizens of England, France, and many other nations, including those of West Africa.

As time passed, this connection became commonplace. Trade and diplomacy with Europeans constituted a normal part of life, not a novelty. Native American peoples got used to new technologies, non-native animals, and European goods and officials. One generation had not known about horses; the next one struggled to figure out how to deal with them; the next one took them for granted, along with chickens, hogs, and cattle. Southeastern Indians quickly got used to raising and eating watermelons and peaches, crops introduced by the Spanish in the sixteenth century. Sometime in the eighteenth century, Cherokees and Delawares learned how to build log cabins like those of Finnish and Swedish settlers. About the same time, Iroquois folks stopped living in communal homes and started living in single-family homes like those of Europeans. These were but a few of the many changes brought about by contact and trade. Throughout America, Native Americans learned to live in "new worlds" that were in many ways unlike those of their ancestors.

In response to contact with new peoples, technologies, markets, and ways of living, American Indians changed their religious traditions. Among other things, new myths arose to explain the differences between Native Americans and newcomers. The first time the Creator tried to make human beings, some Creeks said, the Creator overcooked them and produced Africans. The second time, the Creator undercooked them and made Europeans. The third time, the Creator got it just right and produced Indians. Other people told stories that explained why whites used books while Native American men and women did not.

Just as they assimilated new peoples into their mythic traditions, American Indians integrated novel goods. Eastern Algonquins used colored glass beads and metal objects to enhance ceremonial objects. They turned European stockings into tobacco pouches. Meanwhile, southeastern Indians broke copper pots into pieces out of which they fashioned symbolic jewelry. Thanks to European trade, many more American Indians gained access to metal jewelry, something formerly reserved to a small elite.

American Indians handled many aspects of contact and change well, but problems did arise. After one or two generations of involvement in the beaver and deerskin trades, Native American peoples found themselves quite dependent upon European goods, so much so that they could not conceive of their lives without them. A Wyandot man conversing with George Croghan in Pittsburg in 1759 said, "No Indian Nation can live now without being supported either by the English or French, we cannot live as our Ancestors did before you came into our Country." Farther to the south, Handsome Fellow, a Creek man, said in 1777, "We have been used so long to wrap up our Children as soon as they are born in Goods procured of the White people that we cannot do without it." This type of dependence made Native American peoples vulnerable to European influence in a way their ancestors had not anticipated. To obtain good trading terms or cover accumulated debts, they sometimes ceded land to Europeans, reducing the extent of their hunting grounds.

At the same time, the desire for European commodities, including rum, encouraged American Indians to change the way they hunted. They hunted in other peoples' gamelands, producing regular conflicts, even wars in the north and the south. Everywhere, they took too many animals. This produced catastrophic collapses in the populations of beaver and deer. Even as overhunting threatened the economic foundation of Native American communities, overhunting also eroded traditional spiritual teachings regarding animals. In some instances, Native American hunters took only the skin of the animal for trade, leaving the carcass to rot, unused and disrespected. Such behavior reflected a breakdown in the human-animal relationship and the triumph of market values over spiritual ones.

This pattern was troubling, but another development posed a greater threat. As European settlement expanded and the population of non-Natives soared, colonists became less interested in Indian trade, and far more interested in acquiring Indian land, through any means necessary. During the seventeenth century, English colonists subjugated the Powhatan people of Virginia and the Pequot people of New England and took their lands. During the eighteenth century, it appeared the English might overwhelm the Delawares, Iroquois, Shawnees, Cherokees, and many others. This created the context for new religious movements among Native Americans. These movements sought to halt the expansion of the English and check the spread of Christianity.

In 1751, for example, a young Delaware woman experienced a profound religious vision appropriate for dangerous times. In her vision, God showed her that the divisions between Europeans, Africans, and American Indians were real, not to be overlooked or blurred. Many Delawares, accustomed to life on the "middle ground," had blended European ways with those of their ancestors; one good example was the hunter who shot the bear and yelled at it afterwards. Although he continued to think of animals in a traditional way, he hunted with a musket; he traveled with a German missionary; his people raised hogs. He was not living like his grandfather, nor were his people. Some had converted to Christianity. This was a fundamental mistake, the Delaware woman said.

Her vision revealed, according to a missionary who heard about it from Delawares close to her, that "God gave the white man a book, and told him that he must worship by that: but gave none to the indian or negro, and therefore it could not be right for them to have a book, or be any way concerned with that way of worship." This vision carried great weight among the Delawares. Like many other Native American peoples, they knew that spiritual insight came from such experiences. Taking the young woman's vision very seriously, they convened a great council to discuss its implications.

The council, like the vision, was timely. Many Delawares no longer trusted whites. In 1735, Pennsylvania officials had produced a bogus deed giving colonists a title to Native American lands near the Delaware River. Then, in 1737, the colonists compelled the Delawares to sign a treaty ceding land from a fixed point in Bucks County to as far as a man could walk in a day and a half. To maximize that distance, Pennsylvania officials cleared a path and employed professional runners. Elsewhere, German settlers encroached on Delaware Indian land near the village of Tulpehocken on the Schuylkill River. Everywhere, European traders flooded Delaware villages with rum, luring hunters into addiction and ruin. John Heckewelder lamented that many Delaware men "died of cold and other disorders, which they have caught by lying upon the cold ground, and remaining exposed to the elements, when drunk." Compounding this dreary situation was a fresh assault of smallpox, which struck many Delaware villages in the years following 1748.

When John Brainerd, a Moravian missionary, entered remote Delaware villages in 1751, he moved among people who were suffering, angry, and ready to strike out against the colonists. "Two or three of them seemed to have resentment enough to have slain me on the spot," he later wrote. They told him the message of the young Delaware woman, the visionary who had told them to "destroy the poison among them." They did not clarify whether the "poison" was rum or Iroquois chiefs who had betrayed them or white people in general. But they made it clear that they believed "white people were contriving a method to deprive them of their country in their parts, as they had done by the sea-side, and to make slaves of them and their children as they did of the negroes." A few years later, in 1755, these villagers may have been among those Delawares a Pennsylvania official wrote were "burning and destroying all before them in the county of Northhampton." Killing many settlers and destroying their cabins, they sought to stop the invasion of their land. Theirs was at once a political and spiritual movement.

Other Delawares were drawn to a more peaceful response to the crises they faced. Instead of responding to the prophetess who preached racial separatism and anticolonial revolt, they listened to Papounhan, a Munsee Delaware who lived near the

Pennsylvania–New York border. Papounhan's vision, written down by a visiting Quaker in 1756, was different. "He was formerly a drunken man but the Death of his father" led him to religious reflection.

> He forsook the town and went to the woods in great bitterness of Spirit . . . But at the end of five days it pleased God to appear to him to his Comfort and to give him a sight of his own inward state, and also an acquaintance into the Works of nature—for he apprehended a sense was given him of the virtues, and Natures, of several herbs, Roots, Plants, and trees and the different relation they had one to another, and he was made sensible that Man stood in the nearest relation to God of any Part of the Creation.

Papounhan's vision, in short, combined a traditional Delaware sensitivity to nonhuman persons with a Quaker-like focus on the God-given dignity of humanity.

Of all the types of Christians he knew, Papounhan held the Quakers in highest regard. He said they "walked nearest to what Jesus Christ had required Europeans to do." He urged Europeans to practice what Quakers preached: nonviolence, antislavery, and self-restraint. To his own people, Papounhan advocated more independence from European trade. The people, he said, had grown greedy, too fond of European goods. They had brought sickness on themselves by consuming alcohol. They should mend their ways, learn to live better with less, and stop drinking.

Subsequent prophets reinforced, echoed, and modified these messages. From the mid-eighteenth century until the early nineteenth century, prophets appeared among the Delawares, Senecas, Shawnees, Creeks, and other nations.

These included Wangomend, or the Assinsink Prophet, Neolin, Scattameck, Handsome Lake, Tenskwatawa, Hillis Hadjo, and many others, including some whose names were not written down. Pointing to the loss of game and mounting debts, they declared that God had removed the wild animals to punish Native American hunters for killing animals to trade for alcohol. Hunters, they said, had misused animals and wrecked the spiritual balance. To restore the proper balance, American Indians should pursue an alternative path, one centered on Native American ceremony, not European commerce.

Different prophets described different paths, some peaceful, others not. In 1799, the Seneca visionary Handsome Lake delivered a message of reform, not revolt. The once mighty Iroquois lost many lives during the American Revolution and most of their land afterwards. They responded positively to Handsome Lake. He told the people they could travel a broad and easy road that led to death, destruction, and hellfire. Or, they could process a harder, narrower path that led to cultural renewal and peace. His teachings, now known as the *Gaiwiiyo*, or the Good Word, centered on a moral code. It guided the Iroquois to avoid drinking and gambling, to treat each other well, and to revive other traditional seasonal celebrations. Participants in this movement met in a log structure designed to look like a traditional longhouse. This symbolized neatly their desire to take what was good from Europeans while reinforcing Iroquois distinctiveness and traditions. Influenced somewhat by Christianity, their movement nonetheless reflected long-standing Iroquois values and beliefs. Today it continues to flourish as a distinct religion, an embodiment for some Iroquois of the most traditional dimensions of Iroquois life, and a perennial source of strength to their people.

In contrast to Handsome Lake, who promoted reform, several of his contemporaries advocated revolt. The Delaware prophet Neolin called for a radical break with things European. Based on his visions, Neolin urged his followers to regain their independence, to wean themselves from the worst aspects of the fur trade, and regain the old arts of self-sufficiency. He influenced Pontiac, leader of a massive anti-British uprising in 1762 that involved Anishinaabeg, Ottawas, Potawatomis, Menominees, Hurons, Delawares, Shawnees, Senecas, Mesquakies, Kickapoos, Macoutens, Weas, Sauks, and Miamis. Pontiac's rebels won early battles in the Ohio Valley. However, when diseases such as smallpox weakened Pontiac's forces, English armies overmatched them and won the war.

A few decades later a similar movement arose and united many nations of the Great Lakes region. Advised by a Mohawk prophetess named Coocoochee, American Indians of the Ohio and Great Lakes region fought several battles to rid their lands of the intrusive foreign presence. On November 4, 1791, Miamis, Shawnees, Delawares, Potawatomis, Ottawas, Chippewas, Wyandots, Mingos, and Cherokees defeated in western Ohio a large army led by General Arthur St. Clair. In the battle, 630 U.S. soldiers died. Never before or after would so many U.S. soldiers die fighting American Indians. By comparison, in 1876, when Lakotas and Cheyennes defeated Custer and the Seventh Cavalry only 226 U.S. soldiers perished. Despite this remarkable victory, the U.S. forces proved too strong and in subsequent years prevailed.

But the spirit of resistance rose again. In 1804, a Shawnee

man named Lalawethika awakened from a trance in which he had received a revelation directly from the Creator. This experience transformed Lalawethika, up to that point an alcoholic and a loser. Lalawethika stopped drinking. Taking a new name, he became the prophet Tenskwatawa, the "Open Door." Echoing the messages of previous prophets, he spoke against dependency, alcohol, and land cessions. He disliked the fact that missionaries and other agents of U.S. culture encouraged Native American men to work in the fields growing food crops. In his eyes, only women tended domestic crops full-time. Real men shed blood in the forest.

Sounding an anticolonial note, Tenskwatawa taught that whites were not created by God, but by a lesser spirit, and declared some leaders who had close ties to Americans to be witches. Based on his visions, Tenskwatawa advocated what earlier prophets had requested: the violent expulsion of the Americans from Native American lands. Those who followed him were no more successful than those who had listened to earlier prophets. But like those earlier movements, this one perpetuated and spread the tradition of prophetic resistance to other peoples. Tenskwatawa's brother Tecumseh carried the message to the southeastern nations.

One of the greatest of all Native American leaders, Tecumseh in 1811 traveled among Chickasaws, Choctaws, and Creeks to promote among all Indians cooperation and anticolonial militancy. An early success came among the Creeks. One of the strongest nations in the southeast, the Creeks numbered close to twenty thousand and had never been defeated by Europeans. However, in recent years, they, like many nations before them, were suffering from a decline in game populations and the loss of much of their land base. Georgia had been theirs. Now it belonged to the United States. Most Creeks resented settlers who encroached on their territory and poached their game. Many hated cultural missionaries and governmental officials who maligned the ways of the Creeks' ancestors as "savagery." Tecumseh's message fell on receptive ears. Subsequent to his visit, Creek prophets such as Hillis Hadjo emerged among the Creeks. He gathered a large following of rebel Creeks. To show their solidarity with northern nations, the rebel Creeks danced "the dance of the Indians of the lakes." Within two years, this latest anticolonial movement had attracted nine thousand Creek participants.

Led by prophets, in 1813 Creek rebels killed chiefs whom they viewed as traitors to their people. A civil war resulted. Creeks fought Creeks. When the United States threatened to enter the conflict in 1813, a Creek prophet warned against it. As paraphrased by the U.S. agent, the prophet said, "If whites came among them, the prophets would draw circles around their abode, and render the earth quaggy and impassable. [White soldiers] would be sunk with earthquakes, or hills turned over them." As it turned out, the United States ignored this prophecy and allied with Creeks who did not join the prophetic faction. U.S. officials labeled the prophetic faction the "Redsticks," because of the color of their war clubs. Three U.S. armies invaded Creek country to attack. Supported by their allied Creeks, Choctaws, and Cherokees, the U.S. forces defeated the Redsticks in a series of one-sided battles, several of which should be called "massacres." In the last (and worst) one, the Battle of Horseshoe Bend, fought on March 27, 1814, more than five hundred Redstick men, women, and children died.

One of the few Redstick survivors later said that his fellow Redsticks dropped "like the fall of leaves." This battle, the deadliest ever fought by American Indians against the United States, ended the Redstick revolt in Alabama, but not in the entire region.

Surviving Redsticks fled to Florida and joined their cousins the Seminoles. There, supported by runaway African American slaves, they waged a protracted guerrilla war against the United States. Thus, the tradition of prophetic resistance, dating back at least to the early–eighteenth-century Delawares and more likely back to the seventeenth-century Powhatans, continued to inspire a significant number of American Indians involved in an anticolonial struggle. Guided by their spiritual leaders and great chiefs like Osceola, the Seminoles fought for several decades. Today, some Seminoles in Florida, the Independent Traditional Seminole Nation, like to point out that their people were never completely defeated, that they never really surrendered. From their perspective, the contest continues. They remain unvanquished, a sovereign people in their ancestral homeland.

As for those Creeks, Choctaws, and Cherokees who fought against the Redsticks, victory proved to be bittersweet. Many promises made to Native American allies by U.S. leaders went unkept. General Andrew Jackson, leader of one of the invading armies, forced upon his Creek friends a treaty that took 8 million acres of their land in addition to the 14 million he extracted from the Redsticks. Later, as President of the United States, he would advocate the forcible removal of American Indians from the southeast. By expelling these nations, he would make available for cotton culture their rich lands, facilitating the spread of white settlement and African American slavery. Choctaws,

Creeks, and Cherokees resisted as best they could. During the 1820s, they opposed policies and programs that would rip them from their ancestral homelands. But they carefully avoided stances that seemed too militant or might provoke the United States.

Having witnessed the fatal results of the Redstick revolt, most southeastern Native Americans outside of Florida turned a deaf ear to prophets and militant forms of religion. Religious nonetheless, southeastern Native Americans continued to care about the sacred sites associated with their ancestral dead, the holy places where they emerged from the earth, the spirits of bears, deer, rivers, crystals, snakes, tobacco, and corn. For the first time, however, some of them became actively involved in the religion of the colonists. Dominated by the United States, surrounded by Europeans and Africans, and infiltrated by missionaries, a significant number of American Indians began converting to Christianity. Without forgetting about the Corn Mother, they began praying to Christ, reading the Bible, and going to Christian churches. For better or worse, they helped write a new chapter in the religious history of their peoples.

Among Native American communities, religiously insightful individuals carried great authority. William Bartram, an eighteenth-century English traveler, witnessed the influence of a Native "priest" or "seer" among southeastern Indians.

There is in every town or tribe a high priest, usually called by the white people jugglers, or conjurers, besides several juniors or graduates. But the ancient high priest or seer, presides in spiritual affairs, and is a person of consequence; he maintains and exercises great influence in the state, particularly in military affairs; the senate never determine on an expedition against their enemy without his counsel and assistance. These people generally believe that their seer has communion with powerful invisible spirits, who they suppose have a share in the rule and government of human affairs, as well as the elements; that he can predict the result of an expedition; and his influence is so great, that they have been known frequently to stop, and turn back an army, when within a day's journey of their enemy, after a march of several hundred miles; and indeed their predictions have surprized many people. They foretel rain or drought, and pretend to bring rain at pleasure, cure diseases, and exercise witchcraft, invoke or expel evil spirits, and even assume the power of directing thunder and lightning.

These Indians are by no means idolaters, unless their puffing the tobacco smoke towards the sun, and rejoicing at the appearance of the new moon, may be termed so. So far from idolatry are they, that they have no images amongst them, nor any religious rite or ceremony that I could perceive; but adore the Great Spirit, the giver and taker away of the breath of life, with the most profound and respectful homage. They believe in a future state, where the spirit exists, which they call the world of spirits, where they enjoy different degrees of tranquillity or comfort, agreeably to their life spent here: a person who in his life has been an industrious hunter, provided well for his family, an intrepid and active warrior, just, upright, and done all the good he could, will, they say, in the world of spirits, live in a warm, pleasant country, where are expansive, green, flowery savannas and high forests, watered with rivers of pure waters, replenished with deer, and every species of game; a serene, unclouded and peaceful sky; in short, where there is fulness of pleasure uninterrupted.

CHAPTER THREE

Native and Christian

One November morning in 1818 near Lookout Mountain, Tennessee, a heartbreaking scene was played out between a young Cherokee woman and her parents. Catharine Brown, age eighteen, was a student at Brainerd, a boarding school established by Christian missionaries from New England for the benefit of Cherokee youth. Catharine, in little more than a year of residence at the school, had found a second home and great fulfillment. She had grown fond of the missionaries and their wives. It was as if she had become a member of their families. Their religion fascinated her. Catharine Brown had committed herself to learning about it and becoming a Christian. Now her parents insisted she interrupt her studies and accompany them to a new Cherokee homeland in the West.

Catharine's mother Sarah was crying. A missionary later recorded what happened in the mission journal. According to the written record, Sarah Brown said "she could not live if [Catharine] would not *now* go with them." Catharine, also crying, countered, "It would be more bitter than death to leave." The missionaries, fond of Catharine, and reluctant to lose their first Native American convert, proposed a compromise: let Catharine stay a few more months to complete her education, and then they would arrange her safe passage to the West. But Catharine's father rejected this plan. John Brown said if Catharine did not come now, she would no longer be his daughter. In the end, she relented. After tearful farewells, she left Brainerd, fearing she would never see her Christian friends again "in this world."

As it turned out, John Brown's plans to emigrate fell through and Catharine reunited with the missionaries in April. From then on, her connection to the missionaries would not be broken. Indeed, Catharine Brown the pupil became Catharine Brown the teacher and Christian missionary. In 1820 she founded a school for the Cherokee women of her home valley in northeastern Alabama. Through these and other efforts Catharine helped convert to Christianity many Cherokees, including her parents and siblings. Although her work was cut short by disease—Catharine died of tuberculosis in 1823—she was not soon forgotten. The Brainerd missionaries wrote a book about her life. And generations later, Christian Cherokees living in Oklahoma would remember her as "the Priestess."

Catharine Brown was not the first or last American Indian to convert to Christianity. Over the course of centuries of contact, diverse Native American peoples have become involved in many varieties of Christianity. Anishinaabeg have become Catholics, some Lakota men and women Episcopalians, and many Muskogee Indians Baptists. There have been Iroquois Quakers, Cherokee Presbyterians, Munsee Moravians, Shawnee Shakers, and Hopi Mennonites. There are Navajo Methodists, Osage Lutherans, Paiute Pentecostals, and Mescalero Apache Mormons. There are also Aleut, Yupik, and Tlingit Orthodox Christians. By the beginning of the twentieth century, Christianity had become one of the main ways Native American people expressed themselves religiously. The religion's popularity continued to grow throughout the century until in 1990, two out of three Native American high school seniors claimed Christianity as their religious preference in a poll. Of these, 46.4 percent identified themselves as Protestant Christians and 21.4 percent as Catholic Christians, even though many of them continued to practice their traditional religions as well.

How did Christianity spread so widely among American Indians? The answer is complicated. Various historical paths brought Christianity and Native peoples together. Some of the paths were relatively straight and inviting like Catharine Brown's, others more twisted and painful. Contrasting with Catharine Brown's story was that of Janitin, a Kamia Indian man who lived in the San Diego, California, area during the nineteenth century. He had the misfortune to cross paths with Spanish Christians. Captured while clamming on the beach, he was taken to a mission run by the Franciscan order, baptized, and put to work in a mission cornfield. He might as well have been a slave. Years later he told Manuel C. Roja of his experiences: "Every day they lashed me . . . because I did not finish." When he fled, he was tracked down and recaptured. "They lashed me until I lost consciousness," he said. Such harsh treatment was common in California missions, and helped prompt a revolt of Chumash people in 1824.

Other Native peoples were abused by Christians from England. In colonial New England, for example, Puritan ministers labeled the Pequot Indians "ungodly" and demanded that Christian soldiers destroy them. A massacre of Pequot men, women, and children took place in 1637. A generation later, the Puritan minister John Eliot established segregated communities of Native converts. Most of the converts were Massachuset Indians. In these communities, known as "praying towns," the Massachuset, lured by the promise of peace, gave up control over their lives. The social structure, rules, clothing, manners, architecture, economic activities, and calendar were English, not Massachuset. The intent was to make over Native people in a total way. The message this sent to Native Americans was a very negative one. Telling Massachuset people that they had to change every aspect of their life in order to be accepted by God was like telling them their way of life was worthless, if not evil. And telling them they had to become like the English in order to be saved was racist. Damned if they resembled their ancestors too much, but never able to resemble the English enough, New England converts found themselves trapped in a game they could not win. Without necessarily intending it, the "praying towns" created by Eliot expressed white arrogance and injected self-hatred into the hearts of Massachuset boys and girls.

The "praying towns" did not last very long. In 1675, most Native converts abandoned these settlements and returned to their communities. Nevertheless, their exposure to Christianity did not cease. Their children and grandchildren became more and more familiar with the religion. And as new varieties of Christianity developed, American Indians in New England found new reasons and greater opportunities to participate in the religion. One of the new varieties they found appealing was

Methodism, which emerged at the end of the eighteenth century. Early Methodism was evangelical, which meant that Methodists wanted to share the sacred story of Jesus Christ's holy life with all human beings. Methodists reached out to all classes of people. Among other things, early Methodists preached human equality, opposed slavery, and challenged many of the values held by powerful New Englanders.

These attributes made Methodism attractive to William Apess, a Pequot Indian man born in 1798. An orphan disconnected from his Native heritage, Apess found in Methodist Christianity resources that nurtured self-respect and fed his desire for a just society. The Bible, as he read it, indicated that God was on the side of the outcast, the poor, the disinherited. Speaking as a Methodist, Apess defended the rights and dignity of Native American peoples. At a time when Massachusetts state law banned intermarriage between whites and Indians, Apess spoke in favor of it. The Bible taught him that "God is no respecter of persons." God, he said, did not discriminate on the basis of status, gender, culture, or race. Apess contrasted the "laws of God and nature" with "laws made by man." Apess noted that Jesus was not a Caucasian but a person of color, closer in appearance to Indians than to Europeans. Apess suggested that a dark-skinned Jesus would be rejected by prejudiced white New Englanders. For American Indians like Apess, the Methodist variety of Christianity seemed to support the cause of the oppressed. Like many African Americans, Native peoples found within this kind of Christianity a divine affirmation of their value as human beings. Methodists mistrusted the established elite. They emphasized the inward change of a person's heart as a result of a warm relationship with Christ. Piety and prayer mattered most, not status and education. In Methodism, African

Americans and American Indians found spiritual fulfillment and a potential tool to use against racism. Converting to Christianity, they made Christianity their own. To this very day American Indians in New England practice Christianity in a way that is distinctive from that of their non-Native neighbors.

Living at the same time as William Apess, but far to the south, Catharine Brown had a background and situation very different from his. Apess was an impoverished orphan; she was from an affluent family. Apess did not know his Native heritage; Brown did. His people had been nearly wiped out; her people still controlled a great deal of their original land, and numbered nearly twenty thousand. Like Native American peoples in New England, Cherokees had experienced generations of contact with Europeans and African Americans. Unlike the Pequot people, Cherokees had evaded conquest. This conditioned how they responded to Christianity. They neither rushed to join the new religion nor banned it entirely from their countryside. Rather, they invited missionaries to live among them and carefully considered the messages they brought. Cherokees had the power to decide for themselves whether to join the religion or not. This makes the story of a convert like Catharine different and intriguing. Not disconnected from her tribal tradition and not forced to convert, what was it that drew her to Christianity? What made her want to stay at the mission even though her parents wanted her to leave? The story of this individual Cherokee woman's spiritual journey may help us understand why so many Native people today claim Christianity as their religion. Her story can also illustrate, by contrast, the paths of those American Indians who have not embraced Christianity or had it forced upon them.

Born in 1800 in Will's Valley, a region located in what is now northeastern Alabama, Catharine Brown lived at a time of great danger for southeastern Indians. As the United States increased in population and power, many U.S. citizens became increasingly anti-Indian. Planters and farmers living in Georgia and Tennessee coveted the lands of the unconquered, still powerful Cherokee, Creek, Choctaw, Chickasaw, and Seminole peoples. U.S. citizens missed no opportunity to seize Native lands. As for the Native American peoples of the region, they were uncertain how to resist these encroachments.

In 1811, when some Creek Indians chose a militant approach, the Cherokees, including Catharine, watched to see what would happen to their rebellious neighbors. Indeed, many Cherokees fought against the militant Creeks, joining the U.S. side at the Battle of Horseshoe Bend. Among the Cherokee soldiers were Catharine Brown's older brother and an uncle. After the battle, these men returned to Cherokee country as war heroes. They also served as witnesses to the power of U.S. armies. They had seen the militant Creek prophetic religious movement crushed. They had watched Andrew Jackson's cannons pulverize the fortifications and dwellings of the Redstick Creek village at Horseshoe Bend. Sobered by what they had seen, they brought an important message to their Cherokee kin: Do not fight the United States.

The message was not lost on the young Cherokee Catharine Brown, who was fourteen years old at the time of the Creek war. She decided to seek better relations with the Americans and study their ways. At age seventeen, she traveled one hundred miles northeast to enroll at Brainerd, the new school run by New England missionaries. This was a bold step, but in many ways, her background had enabled her to take it.

Catharine Brown was the child of affluent parents already familiar with the ways of white people. John and Sarah Brown were of mixed Cherokee and European ancestry. Although they did not speak English, the Browns had assimilated a good deal of white people's agricultural lifestyle, blending it with Cherokee horticultural traditions. Like their Cherokee ancestors, the Browns planted corn, beans, and squash. Like their European forefathers, they raised cattle, horses, and hogs. They also held several slaves, a further indication of their relative affluence and extensive degree of assimilation. (Slaveholding had spread among a small elite of the Cherokee people during the last decades of the eighteenth century.) These African American men and women taught Catharine Brown some of the English language and Christian religion, providing her with a good "elementary" education even before she went to Brainerd.

Brainerd was a Christian boarding school designed to remake southeastern American Indians into New England Protestants. This aim shaped nearly every aspect of life at Brainerd, including classroom instruction in secular subjects. Classroom writing assignments consisted of copybook exercises which required young Indians to reproduce moral maxims or Bible quotations. Oral drills focused on the Catechism, a set of statements that expressed the essential truths of the Christian faith. Arithmetic, history, and geography were also taught.

The very design of the institution communicated important values. By 1821, the station consisted of more than a dozen buildings, a garden, and a graveyard. A broad central lane connected the larger buildings. Other buildings were scattered along side paths and situated in surrounding fields or near the creek. Set on a hillside among spruce and oak trees, the station looked like a large farm or very small village. It had the overall appearance of a pleasant college campus in the country. Most important, the design of the station reflected the missionaries' values and goals, particularly their conceptions of proper roles for men and women. Men were to learn how to be farmers, women to be housewives. Female students like Catharine were taught to handle "domestic concerns," to sew, clean, cook, iron, nurse, and babysit. While the boys were in the fields or at the mills, the girls were inside the mission house working at household tasks under the guidance of female teachers and missionary wives. The only other vocational option suggested for girls was that of missionary or missionary wife.

If boys and girls attended different classrooms and learned different practical skills, missionaries taught them the same virtues and provided them with identical religious training. Boys and girls began their days at 5:30 A.M. with prayer and hymns, passed the morning with Bible lessons, and prayed before meals and at bedtime. Throughout the day, individual students would receive words of spiritual encouragement, guidance, correction, and inquiry from vigilant missionaries. Missionaries monitored their students closely for signs of spiritual growth and longing. And they disciplined them for infractions of Christian order, expelling them for sins such as theft or fornication. Designed as a model farm and home, Brainerd was intended also to be a model community, united in Christ.

On July 10, 1817, when Catharine Brown enrolled in the mission school at Brainerd, the missionaries greeted her with mixed feelings. As minister Cyrus Kingsbury interviewed the young woman, he doubted if she would make a good student. He noted that Catharine Brown "had a high opinion of herself and was fond of displaying the clothing and ornaments in which she was arrayed." Kingsbury felt she would not yield to the discipline of the mission school where students not only learned to read and pray, but also to engage in practical manual labor. "She replied that she had no objections to our regulations." Kingsbury told her to think it over, but she was not to be dissuaded. She had traveled a long way from her home in Will's Valley, Alabama, to enroll at Brainerd.

At the time of her arrival, Catharine Brown dressed like other southeastern Indians of her day—colorfully, beautifully, creatively. She blended indigenous and European fabrics, styles, and garments in a hybrid look that embodied in dress the meshing of Native American, African, and European cultures in the Southeast. Catharine Brown's particular indulgence was jewelry. Among other "ornaments," she wore earrings and knob-shaped pins, rings, and a large necklace. According to some of the missionaries, she was inordinately fond of them. As the weeks passed, she attempted to please the missionaries by shedding most of her jewelry. She contributed it to the cause of missions and gave a portion of the necklace to a missionary sister.

These external changes mirrored an inner journey. Catharine Brown was not only altering her appearance; she was reworking her identity. Guided by the missionaries, she learned to practice Christian humility and self-reproach. Catharine Brown prayed frequently, often retreating by herself to the woods to think things over. Throughout the process, Catharine Brown, like most Cherokees, paid close attention to her dreams, which she considered to be messages from the spiritual realm. Indeed, a powerful dream helped her make the transition to Christianity.

It was three months after she enrolled at Brainerd. For ninety days, she had been reading the Bible, saying her evening prayers, and discussing Christianity with her host family. She had not confessed her sin, a necessary step for a person seeking baptism and full membership in the missionaries' church. But, deep inside, Christianity was taking root. The problem was to find a way to reconcile its teachings with her traditional Cherokee religion. The solution came in a dream, which she soon related to the missionaries, one of whom quoted and summarized it in a letter.

> In my sleep I tho't I was traveling and came to a hill that was almost perpendicular. I was much troubled about it, for I had to go to its top. I knew not how to get up. She said she saw the steps which others had gone and tried to put her feet in their steps, but found she could not ascend in this way, because her feet slipped. Having made several unsuccessful attempts to ascend, she became very weary, but although she succeeded in getting near the top, but felt in great danger of falling. While in this distress in doubt whether to try to go forward or return, she saw a bush just above her of which she tho't, if she could get hold it she could get up, and as she reached out her hand to the bush, she saw a little boy standing at the top, who reached out his hand; She grasped his thumb, and at this moment she was on the top and someone told her it was the Saviour.

A rich dream, it blended Christian and Cherokee religious symbols. Mountains were associated with sacred events in both religions. According to the Bible, Moses received the Ten Commandments on a mountain, and Jesus preached his most important sermon from a high hillside. According to Cherokee oral tradition and myths, the Thunder gods resided within mountains. Both religions also described the spiritual quests of individual seekers. Christians read of Jesus wandering in the desert. Cherokees spoke of a sick Cherokee warrior encountering the monster Spearfinger in the woods. Even the savior figure in Catharine's dream appeared to be a hybrid: although identified as the Christian savior, his appearance was that of one of the Cherokee "Little People."

According to a Cherokee story, "the Little People (yunwi' djunsti) are about two and one-half feet tall, are dressed in white, and have long hair. They live in rock slides in the cliffs where one can see 'floors' that they have made—flat places that they keep swept perfectly clean. They can hear whatever you say about them." According to a Cherokee woman interviewed in 1945, "it is a bad omen to see them and death may follow." Yet, there are also traditions that hold that the Little People help children and healers. They "take care of children who wander from their homes, feeding them and teaching them how to use herb remedies before returning them to their parents." Thus, in terms of Catharine's spiritual ascent, it makes symbolic sense that Christ would appear as a Cherokee Little Person. He was there to facilitate her spiritual passage.

The next morning Catharine told her dream to Mrs. Hall, the wife of a missionary. This was a critical turning point in Catharine's spiritual life. To tell someone a dream is to share something deeply personal. To share such a powerful dream with a religious mentor is to invite spiritual guidance. Catharine learned that she could share her inner struggles with Mrs. Hall and other missionaries. Trust grew and a strong bond formed among them. In essence, Catharine became attached to the missionaries. She grew psychologically and emotionally dependent upon them for insight, correction, and inspiration. They became surrogate or substitute parents. As a missionary recorded in a diary, "After this she became more free in conversing on religious subjects & would constantly read her Bible."

As the days went by, the missionaries provided more precise instructions, walking her through the stages of conversion. According to a letter written by a missionary, "One evening she appeared considerably exercised, & as she was about to retire, the duty of prayer was explained & particularly enjoined upon her." Almost on cue, Catharine responded by moving to the next level of faith: contrition, the sense that she needed God's help and forgiveness. "When she supposed the family was asleep, she was heard, probably for the first time in her life, acknowledging her sins, & pleading for mercy." Catharine had learned what it meant to say "I am a sinner." She was well on her way to becoming a Christian. By October 1817, she had become more earnest and desirous of grace, God's saving power channeled through Christ and shared in a church of believers.

In January 1818, Catharine Brown was baptized, becoming the first Cherokee to convert as a result of the mission work at Brainerd. Cyrus Kingsbury, the missionary who had nearly turned Catharine away from Brainerd when she first arrived, preached the sermon. It was based on the New Testament passage from Galatians 3:28—"There is neither Jew nor Greek, there is neither slave nor free, there is neither male nor female; for you are all one in Christ Jesus." In other words, Christianity was supposed to be a religion open to all without discrimination.

Unfortunately for the Cherokees, what might have been true spiritually was not true politically. As the nineteenth century progressed, Cherokees found themselves increasingly mistreated by U.S. settlers and officials. Indeed, Catharine Brown's baptism had been rushed because her father planned to take her away from Brainerd and move west to escape white people. His complaints were recorded by missionaries. "The white people would not suffer him to live here. They had taken his cattle, horses, and hogs, until he had very little left." What was true for Mr. Brown in 1818 was soon true for all Cherokees, rich and poor, Christian and not. Whites entered their land by the thousands during the Georgia Gold Rush of 1829; Georgia extinguished Cherokee sovereignty January 1, 1830. In 1838, the great majority of Cherokees—sixteen hundred people—were forced to move west in a murderous march that cost thousands of lives and displaced midwestern Native American peoples such as the Osages. Cherokees today remember this dreadful journey as the "Trail of Tears."

Catharine Brown did not live to see those dark days. She did not have to walk the "Trail of Tears." She died just as she was beginning her adult career as a professing, indeed professional, Christian. In 1820, two years after her baptism, Catharine Brown had initiated a drive to create a school for Cherokee girls living in her home area. The people of Will's Valley responded with enthusiasm. In an effort that would have won the respect of any hard-working community, "fifty Cherokee men besides boys and blacks assembled, built the house, covered it, and almost completed the floor. Saturday they finished the floor [...] down inside and chinked it and put in the beams." Thus began the final phase of Catharine Brown's life, as a Christian teacher in her Cherokee homeland. This might have been the happiest time in her life.

Unfortunately, at the very moment that she started her career as a teacher, the symptoms of tuberculosis manifested themselves. Aware that she was very sick, but unaware that she would not get better, she mistook her coughing and congestion for a bad cold. She lingered for a few more years. Then, after months of suffering and a final attempt to save her by transporting her to a physician, Catharine Brown died on July 18, 1823, in the area of Huntsville, Alabama.

Catharine Brown's spiritual journey anticipated that of subsequent generations of American Indians. Like her, they were drawn to Christianity for many reasons. As it was for Catharine Brown, conversion to Christianity often seemed an effective way to gain respectability, recognition from powerful whites, and a good education. Like Catharine Brown, converts were able to use their enhanced access to the dominant culture to better promote the causes of their people. Conversion sometimes seemed a good way to expand career options as well as to find a circle of close, caring friends. For some Native women, a religious life as a missionary or nun offered an attractive alternative to marriage and child-rearing. Similarly, for some Native men, ministry and mission work provided the opportunity for travel and prestige.

Like Catharine Brown, many American Indians found ways to reconcile tribal traditions and Christian teachings. This applies to modern Creek Indians. After they were forced to move from Alabama to Oklahoma in the 1830s, Muskogee Creek Indians converted in significant numbers to evangelical Christianity. Today, in Oklahoma, they support twenty-seven Methodist and fifty-three Baptist churches. The sanctuaries of these churches are designed to reflect traditional ceremonial architecture. Traditional Creek town squares were defined by four arbors, rectangular structures that faced inward toward a central fire. In each arbor, men rested on benches. Where they sat depended upon their age, status, and social role. Modern square grounds reproduce much of this design, but so do Creek churches where congregation members sit according to gender and age. Worship in the Baptist churches takes place in the Muskogee language. The Christianity practiced there sounds a distinctively Creek key.

Some Lakota Indians have also found ways to integrate Christianity with their traditional religion. For instance, one of the most famous Lakota medicine men, Nicholas Black Elk, was also a leading promoter of Catholicism. He felt that the seven sacraments of the Catholic Church were similar to seven sacred ceremonials performed by the Lakota people. He saw a hidden unity behind the surface differences. A century later and far from Lakota country, Alex Seowtewa, a Zuni living in western New Mexico, glimpsed a similar unity and sought to make it visible for others. An artist, he has painted the walls of Our Lady of Guadalupe Church with figures representing sacred persons revered in the Catholic faith along with kachinas, deities sacred to Zunis and other Puebloan peoples. His paintings depict thirty blessing kachinas along with Mary, Mother of Christ, and Kateri Tekakwitha, a famous Mohawk convert to Christianity. He plans to paint a large image of Jesus and dress him in classic Zuni clothing. In this way, he says, he hopes "to show that Zuni and Christian spirituality have much to offer each other." Not all Puebloan men and women share this belief or actively practice Catholicism, but most are baptized in infancy in the Catholic Church. Other Native peoples have sought to find a way to respect Christianity alongside their traditions. In 1997 Tom Stillday, an Ojibwa spiritual leader from Red Lake, Minnesota, gave voice to this desire. The first American Indian to serve as the official chaplain of the Minnesota State Senate, Stillday is one of the most highly regarded teachers of the Midewiwin, the Heart Way of Life. This tribal tradition is important to the two hundred thousand Ojibwa people living in

Canada and the Great Lakes states. While its traditions and customs vary greatly from those of Christianity, Stillday perceives important common ground uniting the two religions: "To me, I observe that it's always the same (in both Indian and world religions). We talk about the same Creator, God Almighty himself, and all the spirits we know."

Not everyone thinks universal thoughts like Tom Stillday, draws together gods like Alex Seowtewa, perceives hidden unities like Nicholas Black Elk, or dreams magical dreams like those of Catharine Brown. For many American Indians, the differences between Christianity and traditional religions have seemed insurmountable. Consequently, they desire to keep the religions separate. That is why many modern Creeks refuse to go to church. Instead of joining Methodist and Baptist churches with their kin, they affiliate with ceremonial stomp grounds. At these remote grounds, they celebrate traditional Creek religion by dancing "stomp" dances and performing ceremonials that are many hundreds of years old. Among the Creeks, an individual cannot belong to a church and a stomp ground. A person cannot participate in both religions at the same time.

Contemporary Hopis are not quite as strict, although some of them might like to be. Hopis accept certain religious compromises as necessary parts of living in a world shaped by Christianity. For instance, because they work in regular jobs, Hopis reschedule their ceremonials so that they occur on the weekend. That is the customary time when Jews and Christians worship. Indeed, the whole idea of the "week" is something that comes from the Jewish and Christian traditions. Thus, Hopi religion, at least in terms of the timing of some of its ceremonials, has come to resemble Judaism and Christianity. Nowadays, Hopis also allow their sacred dancers, the kachinas, to dance on

Christian-derived holidays such as Easter, Mother's Day, and Father's Day. And on one occasion Santa Claus, a figure dear to Christians, appeared at one of the Hopis' sacred ceremonies. The two religions, in other words, have not been kept separate; to an extent, Hopis have blended them.

Not all Hopis approve of these developments. Some see the blurring of the boundaries between religions as the unfortunate, but inevitable, fulfillment of Hopi prophecies. These prophecies are modern in origin, provide analyses of contemporary trends, draw pessimistic conclusions, and express these in judgments through religious language. They anticipate a terrible decline in Hopi values. Influenced by these prophecies, some Hopis argue that converting to Christianity is a necessary stage in a much larger drama that will bring fulfillment to Hopis not as Christians, but as Hopis. They anticipate a day when the influence of Christianity will wane.

Still other American Indians have rejected Christianity entirely. This was the choice made in 1733 by Tomo-chi-chi, a Yamacraw leader living in coastal Georgia. Tomo-chi-chi had regular contact with Christians, including immigrants from England and Moravians from Salzburg, Austria. One afternoon Tomo-chi-chi listened patiently to a missionary named John Wesley who praised the Anglican faith and church. However, when Wesley urged him to convert, Tomo-chi-chi reacted harshly. "Why these are Christians at Savannah! Those are Christians at Frederica! Christians drunk! Christians beat men! Christians tell lies! I'm no Christian!"

The spirit of Tomo-chi-chi lives. In the present era, many American Indians continue to view Christianity with suspicion. They link Christianity to the dark story of U.S. racism. They accuse Christianity of involvement in genocide. They note that when Europeans invaded America they did so not as people who just happened to be Christians, but as Christians who felt it their sacred duty to conquer and subjugate non-Christian peoples. Catholic and Protestant colonists dispossessed Native American peoples and attacked Native religions. In the name of God, Christians sanctioned a massive invasion of Native land, enslaved American Indians, slaughtered whole communities, exiled others, imprisoned still others, forced conversion, instilled Indian self-hatred, separated children from their parents, and desecrated Native sacred sites.

Some Native American critics of Christianity also mistrust the Bible, the ancient text held sacred by Christians. They find fault with the Christian story of cosmic creation recorded in Genesis. Why? That story includes the statement: "Then God said, 'Let us make man in our image, after our likeness; and let them have dominion over the fish of the sea, and over the birds of the air, and over the cattle, and over all the earth, and over every creeping thing that creeps upon the earth.'" According to some of the critics, this statement (RSV, Genesis 1:26) places human beings over nature and justifies exploitation of the earth and other living things. Influenced by this text, they say, Christians have behaved in an irresponsible, reckless, and destructive way toward nature and toward peoples involved in earth-based religions.

The Old Testament books of Exodus and Judges also offend Native American critics of Christianity. Why? Those biblical books depict the ancient Israelites' arrival and settlement in the Promised Land of Israel. With God's help they destroyed the land's peoples: "When my angel goes before you, and brings you in to the Amorites, and the Hittites, and the Perizzites, and the Canaanites, the Hivites, and the Jebusites, and I blot them out" (RSV, Exodus 23:23). What makes this story offensive to Native Americans is the use to which it was put in the New World. As Europeans invaded America, Europeans put themselves in the position of a chosen people entering a promised land. As they conquered American Indians, they compared them to ancient Canaanites, the unbelieving peoples subjugated by divine forces. For this reason, Robert Allen Warrior, a contemporary Osage thinker and writer, doubts if the Bible can ever be made entirely friendly to American Indians. Even if it could, he says he would prefer to continue to participate in Native traditions, "to go home to the drum, the stomp dance, and the sweat lodge."

American Indians might be more willing to ignore how the Bible was used against them if the bitterness associated with conquest was deep in the past. Unfortunately, it is not. Contemporary American Indians have heard terrible stories of Christian hypocrisy and cruelty from their own parents and grandparents. Many of these people suffered greatly as children because they were forced to attend Christian boarding schools. Created at the end of the nineteenth century by the United States and Canadian governments, these schools were designed to destroy tribal values and replace them with Anglo-American ones. In many ways, the program of these schools resembled the one that Catharine Brown experienced at Brainerd. But there was one huge difference. Catharine Brown made a free choice as a young adult to enter the mission school. In contrast, the children who attended Indian boarding schools were not allowed any choice. Taken from their communities, often against their parents' wishes, they suffered the terrors of dislocation, lonliness, and cruelty.

Government agents transported children great distances to strange regions filled with Indian-hating people. Beginning in 1879, a federal agent took Sioux boys and girls from South Dakota and sent them to the Indian School in Carlisle, Pennsylvania. There, English-speaking officials stripped the children of their Native clothing and cut their hair, compelled them to wear European clothes and hairstyles, and forbade them to speak their Native languages, beating them if they did. Instead of learning from Native elders about their people's religions, children were taught biblical stories and Christian morality by white people, some of whom also abused the children sexually.

The boarding school experiment hurt Native American peoples. It deeply scarred generations of children, filling them with despair, confusion, and self-hatred. Navajo writer Luci Tapanhonso imagines what it felt like to be a child in one of these schools:

> Sometimes late at night or toward morning when the sun hadn't come up completely, everything was quiet and the room filled with the soft, even breathing of the children; one of them might stand at the window facing east and think of home far away, tears streaming down her face. Late in the night, someone always cried, and if the others heard her, they pretended not to notice. They understood how it was with all of them—if only they could go to public school and eat at home everyday.

Given these bitter memories and the other negative things associated with Christianity, it is no wonder that many Native men and women reject the religion and consider it a bad influence.

Christianity has evoked vastly different responses from Native Americans. This remains true. How could it be otherwise? The story of the spread of Christianity among Native American peoples is a complicated tale with many unexpected twists and turns, outright reversals, and sudden breakthroughs. More than anything, it is a story of contradictions. Because Christianity's spread in the New World is associated with both horrible and wonderful things, it has elicited contrary, even contradictory, responses from American Indians. Some American Indians, conscious of the manifold harm caused in the name of Christianity, have rejected the religion outright. Still others, aware of the powerful and enduring presence of Christianity among their peoples and in the larger culture, have found ways to tolerate it as a necessary evil. Still others have embraced the religion wholeheartedly. They have been attracted like Catharine Brown to the spiritual drama of Christian faith. Or, like William Apess, they have been drawn to the egalitarian promise Christianity sanctions. Many have perceived within Christianity something that affirmed their humanity and fulfilled their spiritual longings. Quite often, they found the religion to resemble Native traditions. They argue with critics who think Christianity teaches hatred of the earth. They point, for instance, to the biblical book of Psalms—"Sing to the Lord, all the earth . . . Let the field exult, and everything in it . . . The trees of the wood will sing for joy" (Psalm 96). They quote Christ's assertion that the stones would cry out to praise God if no one else did. In short, they find enough in the Bible and in their churches to sustain them. For them, there is no insurmountable contradiction in being Native and Christian.

Fig. 1: A participant in the peyote religion beats a ceremonial drum. During the twentieth century the peyote religion spread widely among American Indians in spite of legal prosecution by many states against the ancient faith.

Fig. 2: The Gaan, Apache Mountain Spirit Dancers, celebrate the passage of Apache girls into womanhood at a Sunrise or Girls' Puberty Ceremony in 1947.

Fig. 3: Fifteen hundred years ago, the green table of land on Mesa Verde attracted communities of farmers looking for good places to grow their crops. Around the year 1200, some of them moved from the tabletop to the plateau's sides, where they built handsome stone buildings and large apartment complexes in natural niches.

Fig. 4: The three-thousand-year-old Serpent Mound in southern Ohio, more than 600 feet long, represents the creature most closely associated with rebirth, the skin-shedding snake. Other effigy mounds in the Ohio Valley and the southeast represent other sacred creatures, including birds.

Fig. 5: Wovoka, the Ghost Dance prophet, was also known as Jack Wilson. In January 1892, anthropologist James Mooney photographed him in Mason Valley, Nevada. Wovoka shows some of his spiritual paraphernalia: an eagle feather at his right elbow and the wide-brimmed hat in his hand.

Fig. 6: A 1930 tempera painting by Alfonso Roybal (Awa Tsireh) of San Ildefonso, located in New Mexico, depicts the Harvest Dance, a ritual in which Pueblo peoples acknowledge dependence upon the spiritual forces that bring rain to their crops and food to their families.

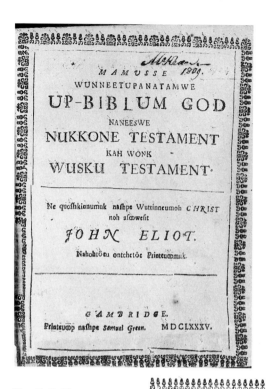

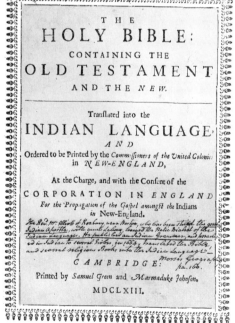

Figs. 7–8: The Algonquian translation of the Bible, a part of John Eliot's attempts to Christianize the Indians of southern New England in the mid-sixteenth century, was used not only for religious purposes but also to establish Puritan political control over Native peoples.

Fig. 9: Missionary Harriet M. Bedell stands with Seminole Doctor Tiger and a small boy in 1936 in Southern Florida.

Notice of Intent to Repatriate

The Department of Anthropology of the National Museum of Natural History, Smithsonian Institution, intends to repatriate 19 cultural items taken from the massacre at Wounded Knee on December 29, 1890, to the Cheyenne River Sioux Tribe on behalf of the Cheyenne River Sioux Tribe Wounded Knee Survivors Association, the Pine Ridge Oglala Sioux Tribe, the Standing Rock Sioux Tribe, and the Rosebud Sioux Tribe. The request for repatriation was submitted by the Cheyenne River Sioux Tribe on behalf of these tribes and the CRST Wounded Knee descendants on June 8, 1995.

The items will be repatriated under Section VII of the NMNH Guidelines for Repatriation, "Objects Acquired Illegally." Since these items were the property of the individuals who were held as prisoners at Wounded Knee, they rightfully belong to their heirs and descendants rather than the individuals who actually obtained them at the site.

Notification of the findings of the Department of Anthropology relative to these cultural items was sent to the aforementioned tribes in May, 1998. Those who wish to express an interest in the items should contact:

Charles W. Smythe
Repatriation Office MRC-138,
National Museum of Natural History
Smithsonian Institution,
Washington, D.C. 20560

(202)633-8132 before July 31, 1998.

Fig. 10: Among the most important crops grown by Native Americans in the east and southwest, corn was sacred, a gift of the Corn Mother and a focus of ritual activities. In most cultures, women, blessed with generative powers themselves, did most of the work of raising and processing maize.

Fig. 11: Once avid collectors of all things Native American, reputable museums now seek good relations with American Indian nations. The Smithsonian Institution routinely advertises its intent to "repatriate" objects, to return cultural items to the nations from which they came.

CATHOLIC INDIAN / INDIAN CATHOLIC

Across the continent and in many different cultures, Native men and women have melded the rites, symbols, and beliefs of Catholicism with their own ancestral ways to create something new and hybrid, a religion simultaneously Native and Christian. Juanita Little (Mescalero Apache), a Franciscan nun, reflects on her own faith journey, "I thought I was a Catholic Indian, but I'm beginning to see myself more as an Indian Catholic." The following is from the book Native and Christian, *published in 1995.*

I'm Sr. Juanita of the Mescalero Apache tribe. I am enrolled in that tribe. My grandfather was captured by a band of Apaches near the Chihuahua area in Mexico when he was six years old. They brought up my father according to Apache ways. My mother is San Juan Pueblo. I really consider myself a real New Mexican. My grandmother was a Spaniard and I'm really proud of that fact because we have a little bit of all the cultures of New Mexico in our family. The Spanish, Mexican, Pueblo, and Apache. Now our younger members in the family are marrying non-Indians and when we get together, we are quite a nation. It is lovely. It is beautiful! We do have, in some instances, trouble within the marriages because those who have married the non-Indians eventually notice the cultural differences. We've had to cope with that as well.

My dream for myself is to build the Kingdom of God among the Apaches.

CHAPTER FOUR

New Religions in the West

On January 1, 1889, a total eclipse of the sun darkened the sky over western North America and spread terror on earth. Alarmed Tövusidökadö Paiute Indians of Mason Valley in Nevada began shooting off their guns. They hoped to scare away the force that blocked the light. They turned for guidance to their weather doctor, a twenty-eight-year-old man named Wovoka. Though ill, he tried to help. Using divination techniques perfected over generations and passed down from his father, he went into a trance or state of unconsciousness. According to many Paiutes, when a healer entered the trance state, it was as if he had died; his released soul could travel to other realms. He could find out what was wrong with a sick person and bring back a healing song. He could divine the patterns of the weather and movements of game. He could glimpse the future or retrieve lost souls. While on this particular spirit journey, Wovoka received a vision of power for all Paiutes, indeed, for all American Indians.

While in the trance, Wovoka "saw God and all the people who had died long ago," he later told James Mooney, a visiting anthropologist from the Smithsonian Institution who wrote down Wovoka's vision. In the other world, the ancestors "engaged in their old-time sports and occupations, all happy and forever young. It was a pleasant land and full of game." According to Mooney's report, after God showed this world to Wovoka, "God told him he must go back and tell his people that they must be good and love one another, have no quarreling, and live in peace with the whites; that they must work, and not lie or steal; that they must put away all the old practices that savored of war; that if they faithfully obeyed his instructions they would at last be reunited with their friends in this other world, where there would be no more death or sickness or old age." Later, as Wovoka left his trance and returned to this world, the sky brightened. It was as if Wovoka had healed not a person, but the Sun itself.

After regaining consciousness, Wovoka recounted to his fellow Paiutes what God had taught him. He described a dance they should perform at intervals for five consecutive days each time. In this way, they would secure happiness and speed the arrival of the new world. Soon many Paiutes were performing the dance, following Wovoka's lead. No longer merely a weather doctor, Wovoka acted now as a Paiute prophet, a leader of a new religious movement.

News of Wovoka's movement spread rapidly. Many American Indians came from nearby regions while others completed longer pilgrimages to hear the new teacher. Joining those Native people thronging to Mason Valley were Mormon settlers from Nevada. Although not American Indians, Mormons attended carefully to all prophecies related to the end of time. Thinking that humanity was in the "latter" or last days, they had organized themselves as the Church of the Latter-Day Saints of Jesus Christ. Moreover, they believed that some "lost" Israelites, frozen in the north, were destined to thaw one day. Wovoka's talk of the land of the dead and the revival of the departed did not seem strange to them. Finally, their prophet, Joseph Smith, Jr., had suggested that a Messiah would appear among American Indians in the year 1890. Everything seemed to fit.

Wovoka agreed that he brought a new and valuable perspective on life. However, he said he was not Christ, a god or savior. Many Indians and Euro-Americans failed to listen and identified him as "the Christ." Word radiated out in all directions: the Messiah had come to earth; He was preaching in Mason Valley.

From the east, delegations of Plains Indians, many riding trains, crossed the Rockies to reach Wovoka. From the west came California Indians who crossed the Sierras on foot or horseback. In Mason Valley, they witnessed men and women dancing for five days at a time, heard the revelations of the prophet, and received symbolic gifts from him—slabs of red ocher dug from a holy mountain, painted magpie feathers, pine nuts, and rabbit fur robes. Wovoka then sent them home to teach the dance to their own peoples. Within months of Wovoka's vision, a new religion was blazed throughout the West. Tens of thousands of Native Americans identified Wovoka as a kind of savior because his movement gave them hope in a time of great change, loss, and stress.

By the late nineteenth century, most American Indians in the West were enduring intensive, if not overwhelming, contact with non-Native newcomers. Even in a remote place like Wovoka's home area, American Indians could not escape. Wovoka lived in the Great Basin, a region of arid land locked between the Rockies and the Sierra Mountains. Even though the land did not lend itself to agriculture, Native American inhabitants found themselves inundated with American and Asian settlers. When Wovoka was a teenager, his father, Numu-tibo'o, fought with American miners and had to flee for his life, leaving Wovoka a virtual orphan. Wovoka found a new home with a white family, the Wilsons. Employing Wovoka as a ranch hand, the Wilsons gave the young Paiute man a new name, Jack Wilson, and taught him their religion, Protestant Christianity. Wovoka, like most American Indians of his day, had no choice but to come to terms with white people and their religion.

In spite of his extensive exposure to white culture, Wovoka championed his people's ways. Like his father before him, Wovoka served the Tövusidökadö people as a weather doctor, one whose dreams give the power to control the weather through spiritual songs, deeds, and words. Even before his great vision, he led the Paiutes' circle dance when it was performed during ceremonies. As men and women moved round and round, processing clockwise and holding hands, Wovoka sang songs celebrating *Damë Apë*, Himself, the mysterious creative spirit behind all things on earth and in the sky. This experience would serve Wovoka well later. He would take the circle dance and make it a key part of the new religion.

At age twenty, Wovoka married a Native American woman named Mary. A Paiute fluent in her people's language, she helped Wovoka build a traditional Pauite circular lodge, a pole-framed structure covered with bulrush reeds. To furnish it, she wove baskets and crafted pottery. To provide food for their family, she and Wovoka gathered pine nuts, collected other seeds and wild plants, killed game, and caught fish. Mary and Wovoka enjoyed a traditional lifestyle blended with a few innovations adopted from their non-Native neighbors. Wovoka used modern guns and ammunition when hunting. He and Mary wore clothes indistinguishable from those of the Wilsons. Wovoka and Mary understood English, but tended not to use it. And, although they did not practice Christianity, they comprehended and accepted some of its beliefs. This hybrid background informed Wovoka's new religion, coloring its content and shaping its reception.

Wovoka's new religion blended together various important religious influences in his world. At the center of the religion was the circle or round dance. Indeed, Paiutes called his religion *Nänigükwa,* which means "dance in a circle." The dance itself was not new and Wovoka had been leading it for years. A dance common in the Great Basin region, it took five days. Normally timed to coincide with the fall pine nut harvest or the spring run of kuiyui fish up local streams, the Round Dance marked times when small bands of people coalesced in a larger group. Such assemblies provided excellent occasions for courting, flirting, partying, and gambling. Dancing added to the festive atmosphere. Yet the Round Dance also served religious purposes. By dancing the Round Dance, Great Basin Indians gave thanks to the mysterious entities that made their existence possible and enjoyable. Directing prayers to *Apë* or "Father," the great spiritual power behind all things, they celebrated the bounty of food they enjoyed and expressed a wish that future needs would be satisfied. Moreover, Paiutes, like most Native

Americans, felt that dancing and singing released creative power and strengthened the positive forces of life. For American Indians of the Great Basin region and elsewhere, dancing could renew a tired or worn-out world.

As he revealed his new religion, Wovoka expanded the theme of renewal to include the dead. The Dance, he said, would bring the living and dead together in a new world. Wovoka's claim was unusual, but he was not the first Paiute to make it. A prophet named Wodziwob had appeared among Northern Paiutes twenty years before. The people he addressed were suffering epidemics of typhoid and measles, land loss, and hunger caused by the increased presence of non-Native settlers. He promised them the return of the dead, the renewal of the earth, a time of plenty to come. His movement spread to many peoples in California, throughout the Great Basin, and north to the northern Shoshone. It disappeared quickly among the Paiutes themselves, but provided a precedent or model useful to Wovoka. Thanks to Wodziwob, Wovoka's startling message of collective rebirth sounded somewhat familiar to Paiutes.

Paiutes were further prepared for Wovoka's vision through contact with Christians, including Mormons, who were dominant in Nevada and Utah. Christians focused on a single omnipresent God, not a pantheon of gods. Similarly, Wovoka did not speak of many gods, but concentrated on one great god, whom he connected to the sun. The Christian religion emphasized the ethic of love and nonviolence. Wovoka's message stressed pacific behavior and contained no hostility toward whites. Christianity contrasted life in an imperfect world with the blissful life to come in a heavenly realm. Wovoka spoke as if a new world was coming that would displace the current, inadequate one. Christians spoke of a comprehensive and violent shift from this world to the next. A catacylsmic Day of Judgment was coming, they said. Christians spoke often of resurrection of the dead, a concept very close to the one Wovoka voiced. Like many nineteenth-century Christians, Wovoka anticipated the new world would come quickly.

Many American Indians recognized the Christian overtones sounded in Wovoka's religion. Some of them referred to his religion as the "Dance to Christ." Northern Cheyennes involved in Wovoka's religion told a story that sounded like something out of the New Testament, the portion of the Christian Bible focused on Jesus Christ and his miracles. According to the Cheyenne story, at a Round Dance performance, buffalo meat kept appearing in their bowls. This was reminiscent of the Bible story in which Christ feeds multitudes of people with a single fish and a single loaf of bread. As this suggests, for Native people living in times defined by increased contact with Christians, Wovoka's religion seems to have enabled them to absorb Christian ideas and stories without becoming Christians themselves. Wovoka's religion provided a Native-based spiritual alternative to the dominant religion of the newcomers.

Wovoka's gospel helped American Indians respond to the ongoing invasion of their land in other ways as well. During the nineteenth century, western peoples had suffered terrible epidemics of smallpox, typhoid, and a host of other illnesses, extensive loss of their tribal lands, and an awful decline in game. By the 1880s, buffalo, once numbering in the tens of millions on the Plains and Prairies, were on the verge of extinction because of Anglo overhunting. This presented a crisis to many peoples.

Old Lady Horse, a Kiowa, explained why. "Everything the Kiowas had came from the buffalo. Their tipis were made of buffalo hides, so were their clothes and moccasins. They ate buffalo meat. Their containers were made of hide, or of bladders or stomachs. The buffalo were the life of the Kiowas." The slaughter of the buffalo, which were absolutely central to the lives of dozens of nations on the Plains, crushed and outraged Indians. A modern Kiowa writer, N. Scott Momaday, equates their slaughter with "deicide," the murder of a god. Witnessing the death of this god, Plains Indians experienced a great spiritual vacuum, a horrible existential hollow. Plenty Coups, a Crow chief, said, "When the buffalo went away the hearts of my people fell to the ground, and they could not lift them up again. After this nothing happened. There was little singing anymore." Sitting Bull, a great Lakota war chief and holy man, said, "A cold wind blew across the prairie when the last buffalo fell—a death wind for my people." For Plains Indians, Wovoka's new religion came at a critical moment.

Consider the bitter experience of the Lakotas, the strongest of all Plains Indian nations. In July 1876 at the Battle of Little Big Horn, or the Greasy Grass as the Lakotas called it, Lakota and Cheyenne warriors defeated the U.S. Seventh Cavalry. By 1881, however, when Sitting Bull surrendered, he could identify himself as "the last man of my tribe to surrender my rifle." Once lords of the northern Plains, Lakotas were reduced to wards of the United States. Vanquished in war, they found their culture attacked in peace. In 1883, the government criminalized the Sun Dance and the Scalp Dance, polygamy, many of the practices of medicine men, the destruction of goods at funerals, and the use of intoxicating substances. Government agents and judges sought to stamp out these "evil practices." In 1888, Agent H. D. Gallagher at Pine Ridge Reservation banned funeral rites important to Lakotas. This alienated the Lakotas because they thought their dead would be ashamed of the living and would have a harder time completing their spiritual journey. Lakotas complained that white men harassed them even in death.

The final blow came in 1889–90. In 1889, U.S. President Benjamin Harrison's administration urged the destruction of the tribal identity of Indian peoples. Agents were directed to teach Indians "to conform to the white man's ways, peaceably if they will, forcibly if they must." To compel Lakotas to stop living in large multifamily camps, officials took drastic steps. They cut the Great Sioux Reservation in half and sold half of the Lakotas' land to non-Indians. They divided the remaining reservation into standardized farms and allotted one farm to each Lakota family. Finally, the government required Lakota children to attend schools to learn English, white values, and the Christian religion. At the time, U.S. policy-makers called this comprehensive program "civilizing" the "savage." In retrospect, it seems closer to cultural genocide. The war against Native peoples had not stopped; it had merely changed form, moving from external physical attack to internal psychological invasion.

To Lakotas experiencing these multiple nightmares of domination, Wovoka's new religion held extraordinary appeal. It was hard to ignore a vision that fueled hope of reunion with ancestors and promised to reverse a dreadful history. Beginning in 1889 and continuing through 1890, Lakotas adopted the new religion with unmatched vigor, reinterpreting it to fit their own religious heritage. They blended the Round Dance with key aspects of the banned Sun Dance. As in the Sun Dance, Lakota Round Dancers circled a sacred tree or pole and stared often at the sun, a traditional purifying ordeal. Because their concern was to bring peace to lost relatives, they called Wovoka's movement *wanagi wacipi*, the "spirit dance" or "ghost dance." Short Bull, one of the Lakota leaders of the movement, said the Ghost Dancers would see their "dead relations" near the sacred tree.

In contrast with Paiute followers of Wovoka, Lakota Ghost Dancers sang fewer songs related to nature and more songs related to the dead and the old way of life. They danced to bring back a lost land full of buffalo and devoid of white people. In another departure from the Paiute Round Dance, Lakota participants wore "Ghost Dance" shirts, muslin cloth garments painted with symbols such as eagles, the sun and stars, rainbows, and red streaks of lightning. Lakotas thought that these shirts provided remarkable protective powers. It is possible that "Ghost Shirts" were based on a Mormon ritual garment said to make its wearer invincible. But Lakotas had their own tradition involving magic protection: Warriors carried shields painted with designs revealed to them in visions. Whether wearing "Ghost Shirts" was influenced by a Mormon practice or derived from the traditional use of magic shields, the practice worried federal agents. U.S. officials misunderstood the significance of these magical garments. Officials on the Lakota reservation mistakenly considered the Ghost Dance militant and Ghost Dancers dangerous.

Throughout 1890, as thousands of Lakota Indians on Pine Ridge and Rosebud reservations danced the Ghost Dance, the authorities became more and more worried. Agents communicated their anxieties to their superiors, describing Ghost

Dancers as "crazy Indians" who might do damage. In response, U.S. President Benjamin Harrison ordered the military to crush "any threatened outbreak." On November 20, 1890, the army entered Lakota country. In a short time, the troops numbered three thousand men. The agent ordered the Lakotas on the Standing Rock and Pine Ridge reservations to stop dancing. Anticipating conflict, newspaper correspondents from the East flocked to South Dakota to cover the story. Meanwhile, on the Standing Rock Sioux reservation, the agent ordered the arrest of Sitting Bull, one of the most important Lakota war chiefs and holy men. When the police entered his cabin on December 15, 1890, a fight erupted. Someone shot Sitting Bull. A grievous blow to the Lakotas, Sitting Bull's death magnified tensions enormously.

Meanwhile, a detachment of troops pursued Big Foot, leader of a band of Mnikowoju Lakotas. When the soldiers found Big Foot's band, they learned that he was very ill. They decided to rest for the night. The next day the soldiers planned to disarm the Lakotas and march them back to Pine Ridge. Mnikowoju families pitched their tents in a creek valley. The soldiers camped around them. The next day, December 29, 1890, when the soldiers began collecting weapons, something terrible happened. Some say a young Lakota man, Black Coyote, refused to give up his rifle. Others say it was Yellow Bird. When a soldier wrestled with him, the gun went off. Hearing the shot, Lakota warriors and U.S. soldiers began shooting at each other. A bloodbath resulted. Using Hotchkiss guns, a new high-tech weapon, the soldiers on the hill sent two-pound explosive shells at the rate of fifty per minute toward the Lakota families. In a few minutes, more than two hundred

Lakotas, including forty-four women and eighteen children, lay dead. Although thirty soldiers died, an early researcher of this event, James Mooney of the Smithsonian Institution, concluded that "there can be no question that the pursuit was simply a massacre, where fleeing women were shot down after resistance, even as they fled to escape." From the wounded and dying, soldiers stripped trophies and souvenirs, including beaded shirts, purses, suede leggings, pipes and locks of hair.

One who heard the guns that day was a young man named Black Elk. An Oglala Lakota camped near Pine Ridge, Black Elk had participated in the Ghost Dance. It had fascinated him in large part because it seemed to fulfill one of his visions. At age nine, spirit men had lifted Black Elk up and shown him wondrous things. Taking him to the very center of all things, they gave him the greatest vision of his life. He encountered the horses of the four directions and spoke with the fundamental powers of the Lakota universe, the Six Grandfathers. He battled and defeated a blue man and a black man, supernatural beings symbolizing drought and war respectively. He learned the hard roads his people must walk and received knowledge, power, and medicine to help them. Finally, the Grandfathers promised Black Elk that one day his people would reach a good place. "Behold the circle of the sacred hoop," the southern spirit said, "for the people shall be like unto it; and if they are like unto this, they shall have power, because there is no end to this hoop and in the center of the hoop these raise their children . . . They put the sacred stick [a cottonwood tree] into the center of the hoop and you could hear birds singing all kinds of songs by this flowering stick and the people and animals all rejoiced and hollered. . . . Depending on the sacred stick we shall walk and it will be with us always. From this we will raise our children and under the flowering stick we will communicate with our relatives—beast and bird—as one people. This is the center of the life of the nation."

For years, Black Elk pondered his vision and attempted to interpret what it all meant. This was not unusual. It often took Plains Indian men and women twenty or thirty years to understand their visions. In 1889, when Black Elk heard about the Ghost Dance, he became excited. Many years had passed from the time of his vision. In the interim, his people had been confined to a reservation. He had traveled through the great cities of the United States and Europe and seen the awesome organizational power of white society. He had nearly given up the dream of seeing the climax of his vision fulfilled. However, when he watched the Ghost Dancers, his hopes soared: the people were circling a sacred cottonwood tree for the purpose of restoring the entire creation. Convinced that his great vision was finally coming true, Black Elk became a Ghost Dancer, helped promote the movement among the Lakota people, and painted holy Ghost shirts for his fellow believers.

On December 29, 1890, when he heard gunfire from the Wounded Knee area, Black Elk responded immediately: "I took my buckskin and saddled up. I had no gun. The only thing I had was the sacred red stick. I put on my sacred shirt . . . This was a bulletproof shirt." When Black Elk reached Big Foot's camp, "I could hear the cannons and rifles going off down there and I could see soldiers all over the hills on each side of the draw. I then depended on my Messiah vision . . . Then I said to the men whom I had led there: 'Take courage, these are our relatives . . . Our women and children are lying dead. Think about this and take courage.'" As he charged in to rescue survivors, bullets hit him but did no harm. "I was bulletproof." Black Elk survived that dreadful day, but after seeing the dead women and children, Black Elk wanted revenge. In subsequent days, he fought in various skirmishes, but the odds were impossible. His band held out for a while, but eventually had to surrender. Black Elk's world had changed forever. His people's dream of a renewed earth had suffered a severe blow at Wounded Knee.

Many years later, a non-Native poet named John Neihardt visited Black Elk, by then an elderly man, and asked him to talk about his youth. Black Elk did so with great passion. The result was a fascinating book called *Black Elk Speaks*. It became the most important book ever written about Native American religion. The book describes Black Elk's great vision, his attempts to become a healer, and some of his adventures with Buffalo Bill's Wild West Show, a horse-mounted drama group that played before urban people in the United States and Europe. The book culminates with a description of Black Elk's response to the Wounded Knee massacre. The last impression is that of an old man who laments the end of his people, the death of their dream. This conclusion is dramatic, even melo-dramatic, but it may mislead readers. Lakota life did not stop in 1890. Nor did Black Elk's religious quest.

After Wounded Knee, Black Elk rejected the Ghost Dance. More than a decade later, in December 1904, he joined the Roman Catholic faith and was renamed Nicholas Black Elk in honor of St. Nicholas. But Black Elk was not content to be just another convert. He became a professional Christian. A member of the St. Joseph's Society, he cared for chapels, taught young people about Catholicism, and led worship services when priests could not attend. Not one to stay home, Nicholas Black Elk traveled to other reservations to missionize Dakotas in eastern South Dakota, Winnebagos in Nebraska, and the Arapahoes and Shoshonis of Wyoming. He became the godfather or spiritual sponsor of several dozen young people. By any measure, Nicholas Black Elk was an extraordinary Christian leader.

Nicholas Black Elk transformed himself throughout his life. This displays the resilient, dynamic way Native Americans respond to religious crises and changes. At bottom, his story seems to suggest that he, like most Native people, did not conceive of religions as bricklike objects that can only butt up against one another. Rather, he saw them as energy fields that can interact like voices harmonizing to produce a song. Born a Lakota, Black Elk blended traditional Lakota practices and beliefs with Wovoka's new religion, which was itself a blend of other traditions. When that union proved unsuccessful, Nicholas Black Elk tried again, and fused Lakota values with Catholic practices. Far from abandoning his original religion, he believed the Lakotas' seven main rituals were echoed in the seven sacraments or blessed practices which fortify the faith of Catholics. For example, just as adolescent Lakotas underwent the vision quest, so young Catholics received the sacrament of Confirmation. Struck by these parallels, Nicholas Black Elk affirmed that the two religions were not at odds. Rather, they pointed to the same truth.

Just as Black Elk survived the massacre at Wounded Knee, so did the Ghost Dance. Although it faded among the Lakotas, it persisted among some groups well into the twentieth century. Alice Kehoe, the scholar who has studied it most closely, found a small community of Lakotas in Canada still practicing

Wovoka's religion in the 1960s. Another scholar, Judith Vander, recorded Northern Shoshone women in Wyoming singing Ghost Dance songs in 1977. A movement that had spread across much of the West, the Ghost Dance did not disappear overnight, but endured in various cultures, guiding a dance, informing a song, toning the outlook of individuals here and there.

In some places and times, however, American Indians resisted Wovoka's religion from the start. This was true of many Comanches, members of a Native nation living on the Southern Plains near the border of Texas and Oklahoma. Comanches first learned about the new religion in the spring of 1890 from Cheyenne and Arapaho neighbors. One of the Arapaho visionaries, a man named Sitting Bull (not the famous Lakota leader of the same name), claimed to have met Wovoka. He shared what he had learned with select Comanches. They were supposed to shepherd their people into the great Indian renewal movement sweeping the West. Some Comanches joined the sacred dance, but most hesitated to do so.

White authorities did not prevent that involvement. Oklahoma officials, unlike their counterparts among the Lakotas, kept an open mind toward the new dance. Lieutenant H. Scott recognized the peaceful nature of Wovoka's teachings. He viewed Comanche participation in the new religion as a prelude to their "Christianization." Having absorbed Wovoka's ethics, the Comanche people would be ready for Christ's commandments. The best thing, Scott advised, was to let the movement run its natural course. Another officer confirmed his judgment, and compared the activities of dancers to the benign ones observed at "an old fashioned Methodist or Baptist church meeting."

Guided by these views, officials nervously observed, but did not ban, the spread of the new religion among the Comanches. Ironically, the religion never took root. Comanches remained largely indifferent to a movement that had absorbed other American Indians. Why?

Comanche indifference reflected the response of their most prominent and powerful leader, Quanah Parker. He opposed the Ghost Dance for two reasons. First, after fighting the white invasion in his youth, he had made his peace with the modern world. Second, he had found another way to fulfill his spiritual needs. The orphaned son of a Comanche chief and a white woman captive, and a friend of white officials and businessmen, Quanah Parker had come to identify strongly with white people and their ways. Later, he would send some of his children to Carlisle Indian School in Pennsylvania so they could become literate in English. In 1890, when he heard about Wovoka's visions, he scoffed. "I want my People to work and pay no attention to that," he told the top white official on the reservation. Instead of crying for a magical renewal of the earth and the return of the buffalo, Quanah Parker urged folks to focus on practical things, to "[d]epend on the Government to help us" learn how to make a living in a market economy. A shrewd entrepreneur who made good money leasing Comanche grasslands to Texan cattlemen, he had found a way to profit from the demise of the buffalo. Quanah Parker had adjusted to the shift from wild things to domesticated animals, from hunting to ranching, from nomadic life to settled existence. During 1890, even as visionaries spread Wovoka's religion, Parker was overseeing the construction of a new home for his growing family. A two-story, ten-room house, it was vastly different from the tepee he had camped in for many years. According to Parker, anyone who got involved in the "Messiah craze" was "crazy." It made much more sense to live comfortably and enjoy the good things modernity had brought.

For all of his practicality, Quanah Parker did have significant spiritual needs. Like the young Black Elk, as a young man Quanah Parker had known the freedom of the old buffalo-centered way of life, loved it, and fought hard to preserve it. In 1874, Quanah Parker had led a large force of Kiowas, Kiowa-Apaches, Comanches, Cheyennes, and Arapahos in an attack on white buffalo hunters camped at Adobe Walls in northern Texas. The professional hide hunters, armed with superior weapons, turned away the Indian forces. They and men like them would soon finish off the buffalo of the southern Plains. Meanwhile, U.S. soldiers conquered the Comanches. In 1875, the United States confined Comanches to an Oklahoma reservation where they suffered diminished freedom, boredom, increased sickness, and intrusive white control. Because of these jarring experiences, the Comanches, like the Lakotas, needed to adjust their religious life in fundamental ways. They did so during the 1880s by adopting a new religion—the peyote religion. The foremost champion of this new religion among the Comanches was Quanah Parker, an ex-warrior turned businessman.

How Quanah Parker first learned of the peyote religion was not written down. One story focuses on the years just after 1875. For the first time experiencing peaceful contact with whites, he began to search for his mother's family, to reclaim that part of his identity. When he learned that her name had been "Parker," he adopted it as his own. Then, he traveled to

Chihuahua, Mexico, to visit his mother's brother, John Parker. There a bull gored Quanah Parker. When the wound became infected, the young man seemed on the verge of death. After it became clear that Anglo doctors could not help him, his grandmother hired a *curandera*, a Mexican Indian healer. Perceiving that he was an Indian, she dosed him with a very bitter tea.

Restored to health, Quanah Parker learned that the tea had been made by boiling a green cactus called peyote. Peyote, it turned out, was much more than a medicine. Peyote was a sacred food celebrated in a venerable Indian religion that predated Columbus. For centuries, participants in the religion had consumed the cactus in a ritual way. They considered peyote a sacrament, a blessed substance that connected them to the gods. During the sixteenth and seventeenth centuries, when Spanish colonial authorities in Mexico tried to suppress the peyote religion, participants hid it. It survived among Indians living in northern Mexico, where peyote grows naturally. It was there or near there that Quanah Parker first experienced peyote's power.

With the help of the *curandera*, Quanah Parker learned much more about the sacred plant and attended a peyote ceremony, an all-night ritual involving songs, prayers, and consumption of the sacred plant. When the bitter button-shaped growths on the peyote plant are eaten whole or imbibed in a hot tea, they produce a host of unpleasant symptoms. Summarized by scholar Christopher Vecsey, these include "nausea, dizziness, choking, the pains and shortness of breath, the hunger, cramps, and tremors, accompanied by restlessness, anxiety, depression, agitation, fear of death and dissolution." To consume peyote, then, requires one to undergo an ordeal few would desire. Some describe it as "self-torture." What helps to make the experience tolerable is that these unpleasant effects are followed by more enjoyable ones. Summarized by Vecsey, these include "euphoria, peace, contentment, contemplation, exhilaration, and pleasant fantasies that can last for many hours." The experience of feeling terrible, then blissful may have reminded Quanah Parker of the vision quest, one of his people's main spiritual practices. The vision quest required an individual to undergo a solitary physical ordeal in order to become worthy of a vision and the power it provided. In any case, Quanah Parker did not shy away from peyote merely because it involved a preliminary ordeal.

From people involved in the religion, Quanah Parker learned the oral tradition surrounding peyote, including how human beings had first experienced the plant's spiritual power. Once, a story related, there was a person in desperate need, someone separated from her tribe, lost, or grieving the death of a loved one. At a critical moment, peyote appeared and revealed its healing power. It cured totally, instantaneously, and miraculously. Many dramatic stories sang the praises of peyote.

These stories mirrored the individual experience of Quanah Parker with the holy plant. An orphaned youth, he too had been mourning a lost relative, separated from his people, and ill. He too had known nothing of peyote, and yet, peyote had healed him. Indebted to the sacred medicine, Quanah Parker became a leading advocate of the peyote religion among the Comanches. Acting as a ceremonial leader or "Road Man," he helped transmit it to many other Native peoples residing in Oklahoma and beyond. Indeed, Quanah Parker's influence among peyotists was so great that the ceremony he taught became known as the Quanah Parker Way.

Also known as the Comanche way or the Kiowa way, the

Quanah Parker rite was more widely known as the Half Moon ceremony. This ceremony, primarily a male affair, took place within a tepee, usually beginning on Saturday evening and not ending until the next morning. Male participants sat in the tepee. Women stayed outside, unless they were sick, in which case they were admitted for a portion of the ceremony. The name "Half-Moon" referred to the shape of the altar, a mound of earth designed to curve around a small fire-hole and point toward the east. Once the Road Man had sculpted the altar, he placed on it a bed of fragrant herbs in the form of a cross, then rested on the herbs a large peyote button. He spread wild sage around the sides of the tepee to provide a good place for the men to sit. The Road Man also procured ceremonial objects, peyote buttons, tobacco, food and water. His wife prepared meals for the participants.

The liturgy or order of worship involved many phases, including the lighting of a fire in the fire hole, prayers, the ritual consumption of peyote buttons, songs, a midnight break for the weary, a rite involving water and an eagle feather, prayers for the sick, ceremonial smoking of tobacco, a cooling drink of blessed water, additional consumption of the sacrament, an early breakfast consisting of water, corn, meat, and fruit, a discussion of the ceremony and rehearsal of new songs, and finally, a great feast prepared by the wives of the participants.

Such a ceremony had a powerful effect on its participants, healing bodies and spirits. Confirmed alcoholics stopped drinking, sick children revived, and almost everyone felt closer to the sacred powers. C. S. Simmons, a white convert to peyote and friend of Quanah Parker, described a high point from one of Parker's peyote meetings in the following way: "At about three o'clock in the morning, the 'silent hour' and the time of the greatest manifestation of power, Quanah, the leader, knelt before the altar and prayed earnestly. Then, taking the eagle feathers in both hands, he arose to his feet. I saw at once he was under great inspiration. His whole personality seemed to change. His eyes glowed with a strong light and his body swayed to and fro, vibrating with some powerful emotion. He sang the beautiful song 'Ya-na-ah-away' (the eagle's flight to the sun), in a most grand and inspiring manner. Then all sang together in harmony. They prayed to God and to Jesus, and sang of a 'narrow way.'"

The Half Moon ceremony sometimes incorporated aspects of Christianity. Nevertheless, Quanah Parker insisted on a distinction between his ritual practice and those of Christian churchgoing folks. "The white man goes into his church house and talks *about* Jesus, but the Indian goes into his tipi and talks *to* Jesus." Other Half Moon peyotists insisted it was not Jesus whom they spoke to, but the Great Spirit and Mother Earth. Meanwhile, still other peyotists, followers of the Cross Fire branch of the peyote religion, saw themselves first and foremost as Christians. Far more than Half Moon peyotists, Cross Fire believers employed Christian language, the Bible, and other Christian symbols in their ceremonies. Cross Fire peyotists equated peyote with the "road to Jesus Christ."

Just as Indians practiced multiple versions of the Ghost Dance, some more explicitly Christian than others, so they sanctioned diverse interpretations of the peyote religion. As the religion spread to new nations and regions, such pluralism became inevitable. Or did the existence of divergent approaches help the religion spread to new areas, each variety appealing to a different constituency? In either case, as American Indians faced the new challenges of postconquest life on the reservation, thousands of them found in the new religion a persuasive and positive way to renew themselves spiritually. For those not drawn to the Ghost Dance, as well as for some who were, the peyote religion provided a cherished path to peace.

As the peyote religion spread northward, some U.S. officials and missionaries sought to suppress it, repeating the behavior of hostile Spanish colonial officials. U.S. officials and missionaries wanted American Indians to become Christians, not peyotists, and they considered peyote itself to be an illegal intoxicant. They took a variety of steps to cut off the peyote supply and undermine the religion. They confiscated shipments of peyote buttons. They bought most of the supply from merchants in Laredo, Texas, and burned it. They fined people caught with the sacred plant. They threatened peyote leaders with legal action. They sent spies to peyote meetings, seeking to find out who was participating. They broke up other meetings and arrested participants. In 1886, on the Comanche-Kiowa reservation, Agent Lee Hall threatened peyotists with "loss of annuity goods, rations, and the grass money from the leases." Other opponents solicited stories that would show how peyote harmed people. They lobbied hard against the substance with state legislators and the Bureau of Indian Affairs, comparing peyote with "Marihuana and Hashish." In the end, their efforts to squelch the religion were no more successful than those of Spanish authorities from prior centuries. In spite of their harassment, the peyote religion continued to attract Native American participants, a testimony to the appeal of the religion itself and the tenacity of its adherents.

In Oklahoma, no one defended peyote more effectively than Quanah Parker. He sent agents to Mexico to purchase thousands of buttons for redistribution. He taught the religion to Delawares, Caddos, Kansas Potawatomis, Cheyennes, Arapahos, Poncas, Otos, Pawnees, Osages, and others. He explained the religion to non-Native outsiders, including Christian clergy. He converted the local blacksmith, one C. S. Simmons, to the religion by healing him of a chronic illness. He traveled to the Oklahoma Constitutional Convention in 1907, where, along with other peyotists, he argued against an anti-peyote bill, identified peyote as an herb, and praised its healing properties. Later, when William E. "Pussyfoot" Johnson, a special federal agent combating drug and alcohol use among Indians, confiscated a major supply of peyote buttons, Quanah Parker persuaded a congressman and a senator to intervene. Because he was so well connected, fairly affluent, and widely respected by whites, Quanah Parker proved an able champion for the new religion, and it flourished.

In 1918, Oklahoma peyotists organized the "Native American Church" (NAC). Its stated purpose was to promote "the Christian religion with the practice of the Peyote Sacrament." By providing an institutional identity for the religion, the NAC helped unite those involved in it, providing them with greater strength than they would have in isolation. Soon the NAC was incorporated in many states. By equating the religion with a Christian denomination, the NAC helped make peyote seem less alien to non-Natives familiar with organized religions. Although many states and some tribal governments banned the religion, it gained some protection from courts and Congress, often because of NAC efforts.

Today, the NAC is strongest in Navajo territories in Arizona and New Mexico, despite the fact that it was banned there for a quarter of a century. Peyote provides contemporary Navajos with a worship practice suited to the constraints of modern life. Forced by the government to rely less upon sheep for their livelihood, Navajos have moved away from traditional homes in rural locales to work in larger towns and cities, with several consequences. Navajos spend less time with an extended family network and more time in a nuclear family. Children spend their days in school and pass less time with their grandparents. As a result, many of them do not learn the Navajo language and cannot understand the songs, chants, and prayers of Navajo medicine men. They cannot be expected to participate as fully in traditional religious ceremonies. Finally, families can no longer afford to feed the large groups of people who attend traditional curing ceremonies or to sacrifice the time these complex ceremonies require. They crave simpler, less expensive ceremonies such as those of the peyote religion. Its ceremonies require less knowledge of Navajo language and cost less than the more elaborate traditional Navajo ceremonies. This is not to say that peyote has displaced traditional religion entirely. A third of the Navajo people carry on their ancestors' religious traditions. But for many of these, the peyote religion provides an important supplement to their spirituality. For another third of all Navajos, participation in the peyote religion constitutes their primary spiritual activity. In all, as many as half of the Navajo people are members of the NAC. It suits the conditions of modern Navajo life. And, as it has for generations of American Indians, it provides uniquely direct access to God, something Navajo peyotists value.

Jack Hatathlie, a Navajo Road Man who traces his teaching back to Quanah Parker, sees a bright future for his religion. "I believe the Native American Church is the religion for our young people. It's not complicated; it's very simple . . . Everybody is stressing education so all can be able to make it in today's society. . . . This way of praying, the NAC, is good for young people. If you are honest with the medicine, it will guide and help you." Others agree, emphasizing how they find no limits to what they learn through this religion; they do not grow bored with it; it continues to open them to richer insights, helping them see greater meaning in life, hidden connections. "Everything is acknowledged in there," Ella, Jack Hatathlie's daughter, emphasizes, "like sometimes you'll say 'Mother Peyote,' or 'Father Peyote,' 'the Fire,' 'Grandfather Fire,' 'Grandmother Poker,' 'the Fire Poker,' 'Our Mother the Water.' Indian people think everything is interrelated, that's why everything is as a whole in there."

In spite of the beauty and purpose participants find "in there," outsiders have banned and abused the peyote religion. Its teachings and rituals remain poorly understood by most Americans. Peyotists continue to suffer discrimination. The 1990 Supreme Court decision in *Oregon v. Smith* dealt peyotists a serious blow. This case involved an American Indian fired from his state job because of his participation in worship services of the NAC. When he was denied his unemployment compensation—money paid by the state to workers temporarily out of work—he sued the state seeking relief through the court system. The case made its way up to the Supreme Court. In its decision, the Court said what had happened was permissible. Because the agency the man worked for did not want its employees to consume "drugs," it could legally fire a man for consuming peyote in NAC ceremonies. It did not matter that he consumed the cactus as part of a recognized religious tradition. What mattered most, the Court said, was that the state agency claimed to have a vital interest in controlling certain off-the-job activities of its employees. The fact that those behaviors were religiously governed or motivated carried no significant weight. Logically, this decision means a state, waging a war on alcohol, could fire Catholics for consuming a small portion of wine during Communion, a central ritual of worship in their church and a key part of their religion. By the same token, another state, in the interests of public health, could ban the production of kosher food, something essential to the practice of Orthodox Judaism.

Despite centuries of efforts to suppress it and recent instances of discrimination, the peyote religion remains a vital part of Native American life. Nurturing almost two hundred thousand American Indians, peyote continues to help those struggling with a lack of meaning in ordinary life, racism, illness, negative self-images, alcohol and drug abuse, and a host of other problems. It sustains and inspires those seeking to walk with dignity and purpose, enabling them to live life more fully and love existence more deeply. So long as Native American men and women seek to understand things within a spiritual perspective, it is likely the peyote religion will thrive. With roots that extend back before Columbus, the peyote religion will continue to salve the hurts and inspire the hearts of American Indians well into the future.

For hundreds of years a debate has raged over how to classify peyote, a cactus that grows naturally in northern Mexico. For those involved in the Native American Church, peyote is a sacred substance that brings one into intimate contact with the divine, much like wine does for Catholics who consume it during the Mass. For some state authorities, however, peyote is just another intoxicant or even a narcotic, on par with marijuana and cocaine. What follows is the testimony of Francis La Flesche (Omaha) before Congress in 1918.

When I went among the Osage people, some of the leaders of the peyote religion were anxious for me to attend their meetings, and wishing to know what effect this "medicine," as they called it, had upon each individual, I accepted the invitation. I attended a meeting at which the gentleman who has just spoken to you, Mr. Arthur Bonnicastle, was present, and sat with him. At about 6 o'clock in the evening the people entered their "meeting house" and sat in a circle around a fire kindled over some symbolic figures marked in the center of a shallow excavation in the middle of the room. The peyote was passed around, some of it in pellets of the consistency of dough, and some prepared in liquid form. The drum was ceremonially circulated and accompanied by singing. From all that I had heard of the intoxicating effects of the peyote I expected to see the people get gloriously drunk and behave as drunken people do. While I sat waiting to see fighting and some excitement the singing went on and on and I noticed that all gazed at the fire or beyond, at a little mound on top of which lay a single peyote. I said to the man sitting next to me, "What do you expect to see?" He said, "We expect to see the face of Jesus and the face of our dead relatives. We are worshiping God and Jesus, the same God that the white people worship." All night long the singing went on and I sat watching the worshipers. It was about 5 o'clock in the morning when suddenly the singing ceased, the drum and the ceremonial staff were put away, and the leader, beginning at the right of the door, asked each person: "What did you see?" Some replied, "I saw nothing." Others said, "I saw the face of Jesus and it made me happy." Some answered, "I saw the faces of my relatives, and they made me glad." And so on, around the entire circle. I noticed that there were only a few who had been able to see faces, the greater number of the men and women saw nothing. It was explained to me by the leader that these revelations come quickly to those whose thoughts and deeds are pure. To those who are irreverent, they come slowly, although they may come in time. This meeting, as well as others that I have been permitted to attend, was as orderly as any religious meeting I have seen in this and other cities . . .

I do not know about the medicinal qualities of the peyote, whether it can cure consumption or any other disease that the human flesh is subject to, but there is one disease it has cured—the disease of drunkenness.

About 15 years ago, my people passed through an extraordinary experience. White men came among them, generally known as "boot-leggers," to sell whisky and lemon extract. What the whisky was made of I don't know—these "boot-leggers" would sell anything that could produce drunkenness. My people fell into the habit of using this stuff—manufactured by white people—and kept using it until they were in the very depths of degradation. In their drunkenness they attacked men, women, and children. Crimes have been committed that have never been heard of, crimes that have gone unpunished, and white people and Indians alike became afraid to go out at nights on the road for fear of meeting drunken Indians. There came a time when there was a lull in this storm of drunkenness, and after awhile we heard that the peyote religion had been adopted by the Omahas, and there were not as many drunkards as before the introduction of it.

Practically all of those of my people who have adopted the peyote religion do not drink. The peyote plant does much toward destroying the appetite for intoxicants. Moreover, any use of spirituous liquors is forbidden by the teachings of the new religion.

I have a respect for the peyote religion, because it has saved my people from the degradation which was produced by the use of the fiery drinks white people manufacture...

CHAPTER FIVE

Homecoming

L one Wolf, an Odawa Indian in the Great Lakes region, starts each day mindful of his moral responsibilities to the world around him. "I wake up every morning and go outdoors to a little place in the yard and, facing east, give thanks and offer tobacco to the *manidos* for the good morning." Like his Algonquin ancestors who offered tobacco to the spirit of the wind before canoeing across a lake, Lone Wolf cultivates a good relationship with the *manidos*, the nonhuman power persons who enliven the Odawa world. Attending to their feelings, giving thanks for their blessings, Lone Wolf expands his own moral sense to embrace wider circles of concern.

As he explained in the early 1990s to anthropologist Melissa Pflüg, "I see myself standing here in the center." Surrounding him are ever larger, inclusive circles consisting of his family, his clan, his people, all Native American peoples, all human beings, and all ancestors. "Out from them are the animals and plants. Then comes A-ki [Earth], Mishomis [Sun] and Nokomis [Moon]. The next largest circle are the great powers, or *manidos*. It's everyone's job to keep these relationships held together, across all the circles, and from their own place as center."

By offering tobacco each morning, Lone Wolf does part of his "job." Through this act and many others, he seeks what the Odawas call *pimadaziwin*, the Right Path. Aiming for the Right Path, he and other traditional Odawas undergo individual vision quests and engage in collective ceremonies, including pipe ceremonies, sweat lodges, dances called powwows, feasts, Elder Councils, and Spiritual Get-Togethers. These activities help neutralize conflicts among people, strengthen the memory of the beloved dead, empower men and women struggling with domestic abuse and alcoholism, and remind people of the heartbeat of the earth. Ideally, these ceremonies enable Odawas to enjoy a robust moral life, one mindful of the *manidos* and concerned about the community.

Far to the west in Arizona, religious ceremonies help sustain another Native American people. Unrelated to the Odawas, the Western Apaches inhabit a very different landscape, a largely arid desert punctuated by beautiful mountains. The mountains provide welcome relief and a strong contrast to the desert. Topped with clouds, veined with springs, cooled with wetlands and streams, and shaded by spruce and fir trees, these peaks, until recent times, provided Apaches with food, medicine, building materials, and other necessities. Most important, to many Apaches, these mountains hold sacred value.

Located there are secret shrines, ancestral burials, magic stones, and supernatural beings. Franklin Stanley, an Apache medicine man, elaborated, "I know the songs that are sung at our holy ground, and there are songs about Mt. Graham that are an important part of our religious practice. There are herbs and sources of water on Mt. Graham that are sacred to us. Some of the plants on Mt. Graham that we use are found nowhere else. These plants are important to our spiritual practices and healing . . . The mountain is part of spiritual knowledge that is revealed to us. The mountain gives us life-giving plants and healing . . . Our prayers go through the mountain, to and through the top of the mountain."

According to Apache creation stories, some of the most important spirits, the Gaan, live in mountain caves. Some Apaches locate these caves on Mt. Graham, the peak they call Dzil Nchaa Si An, which means "Big Seated Mountain." Others point to the Superstition Mountains. The Gaan descend periodically from the mountains to heal, educate, purify, and bless Apache life. The Gaan play a critical role in the Apache Girls' Puberty Ceremony, a central event in young women's lives. During the ceremony, four talented Apache men perform a dance. The men wear painted headdresses that symbolize the Gaan. Each spirit is associated with one of the directions of the earth. Together, the four directions symbolize the entirety of existence. This is appropriate because Apaches believe female puberty has universal significance. Menstruation matters. To become a woman is to participate in a timeless power that can bring good things to the whole cosmos. Just as many Native nations throughout history gave high status to women, so Apaches celebrate and rely upon women's moral leadership, physical strength, and spiritual power.

During the ceremony, the girls wear beautifully beaded buckskin dresses and beaded moccasins. Some girls' dresses are as elaborate, expensive, and symbolic as wedding dresses. Some dresses have been blessed by having an honored elder woman sing over them for two months. Most feature symbols including the morning star, the crescent moon, the sun, and rainbows. The dresses copy the one worn long ago by an Apache goddess of life, White Painted Woman. According to Apache oral tradition, long, long ago, when everything was being created on earth, White Painted Woman received the gift of menstruation. During the puberty ceremony, Apaches celebrate the fact that young women have received this gift. To dramatize their connection to the goddess, the girls perform gestures and deeds that replay the actions of White Painted Woman. Because the girls radiate healing and prosperity, people gravitate to them. Witnesses of the ceremony gaze upon the girls in their ceremonial dresses, touch objects they have handled, and consume foods they have blessed.

The puberty ceremony inspires the girls, their relatives, and the community in general. A Christian minister who observed a version of the ceremony on the Mescalero Indian reservation in southern New Mexico considers it "one of the most beautiful things that could ever happen. Imagine this: for 12 days—4 days precelebration, 4 days of celebration, and 4 days following—this girl is a special person. All this time, the family and the community is praying for her. It's very spiritual . . . I look at that and think it's something that every kid in the world should grow up with. . . . I don't know if there's anything comparable in the white dominant society." A festive and warmhearted spirit unites all who attend. Among the Mescalero Apaches, the ceremony climaxes a four-day festival that combines ancient ritual activity with a rodeo, a parade, a family reunion, and a communal celebration. Folks welcome strangers, visit friends, and consume big meals of beans, chili, fry bread, mesquite pudding, coffee, and Kool-Aid. The Apache girls depart from the ceremony feeling they have become important persons with special powers and new responsibilities. They have contacted sacred realities. The mountain-dwelling spirits have danced for them and their people.

Thinking of the Gaan and their importance to his people, Franklin Stanley became worried in the 1980s when a new construction project began on Dzil Nchaa Si An. The project would place a new observatory on the mountain. Astronomers at the University of Arizona and other institutions believed the mountain provided an ideal location for their high-tech telescopes, a site free of the light pollution of Sunbelt cities, high enough to take advantage of a thinner atmosphere, and yet not too far from Tucson and the University of Arizona.

Stanley feared the project would disrupt Apache religious life. "The mountain is like a gateway or river," Stanley said, "and putting the telescopes on top of the mountain is like putting a dam on the river . . . The 'Gaan' live on Mt. Graham. . . . If you take Mt. Graham from us, you will take our culture. . . . If you desecrate Mt. Graham it is like cutting off an arm or a leg of the Apache people."

Not all Apaches agreed. Norma Jean Kinney, a San Carlos Apache, declared, "I've lived here all my life and I've never heard anyone say that Mt. Graham was sacred, until Franklin Stanley began saying it." William Belvado, also an Apache, concurred. "One mountain just isn't that important . . . The observatory isn't going to destroy our culture. . . . We have maybe 80 percent unemployment, and it will mean jobs. . . . When

Indians attack the university, it's like saying that education itself is not an Indian value, that it's un-Indian to learn. We should be working on education, the economy, programs for the elderly."

Still other Apaches agreed with Stanley. Ola Cassadore Davis, raised on San Carlos reservation and the daughter of a famous Apache spiritual leader, shared his concerns. In October 1989, she experienced a series of important spiritual visions related to the mountain. While on a vision quest, she saw herself clutching the east side of Dzil Nchaa Si An. A white man grasped the west side. Joining hands, they sheltered the entire range. Because of this vision and others Ola Cassadore Davis consulted with Stanley. He told her "The Creator, he's telling you the true things, the way it is." Accordingly, Ola Cassadore Davis helped create the Apache Survival Coalition, a unique alliance of Native Americans and non-Native environmentalists fighting the construction project which would harm a rare subalpine forest ecosystem.

The coalition launched a publicity campaign to shame and embarrass backers of the project. Apaches gave their side of the story in newspapers and on television, in the offices of congressmen, and among friends living in the cities of the United States and Europe. Environmentalists, members of the American Indian Movement (a group organized in 1968 to protest governmental abuses of Native peoples), and Apache elders and medicine men worked together, united by the slogan: "Mt. Graham—Sacred Mountain, Sacred Ecosystem."

At first, their efforts succeeded. In 1990, the San Carlos Apache Tribal Council condemned the observatory. Studies established that better sites existed for the observatory. Institutions that had planned to support it withdrew. These included the Smithsonian Institution and several major U.S. universities. Yet the University of Arizona, which supports the largest number of astronomy teachers and students in the country, remained committed to it. Politically well connected and economically powerful, the university loomed as a formidable adversary. On December 7, 1993, the university clear-cut trees at a site on the mountain. By 1996, the builders had constructed two telescopes and the project had found additional institutional support. In 1997, an Apache woman praying on the site was arrested for trespassing.

Similar contests over land have erupted all across the United States and the rest of North America, as development accelerates, road construction spreads, and tourism increases. These contests reveal religious differences not only between members of the dominant non-Native culture and those of Native American peoples, but within Native American communities as well. Native American individuals differ widely in their understandings of the spiritual importance of the land. Some consider land unimportant, believing religious fulfillment hinges only on their faith in Christ. Many, however, associate spiritual power with specific places, a point stressed by Vine Deloria, Jr., the Lakota author of *God is Red* and several other books dealing with Native American life. As Deloria states, traditional Hopis, Navajos, Pueblos, and other Native American peoples cherish the places where, according to their traditions, they "completed their migrations, were told to settle, or . . . where they first established their spiritual relationships with bear, deer, eagle, and other forms of life who participate in the ceremonials" they practice. Many Lakotas revere a site called Buffalo Gap located in the Black Hills of South Dakota. Their traditions say human people and buffalo people emerged from the earth in primordial times at Buffalo Gap.

Even more sacred to the Lakotas is Bear Butte, South Dakota. It is among those few places that are "Holy in and of themselves," according to Deloria. At such places, ceremonies can be performed that benefit all of humanity. These ceremonies complete the "largest possible cycle of life," Deloria says, and help the cosmos become "thankfully aware of itself." At such places, human beings can communicate with higher spiritual powers. Larry Red Shirt, Lakota spiritual leader, compares Bear Butte to Mt. Sinai, a Middle Eastern site where, according to a story in the Bible, God spoke to Moses, a great Jewish hero: "The original instructions of the Lakota was given by the Creator on a sacred mountain similar to the way the Ten Commandments were given to Moses on [Mt. Sinai]. . . . The Lakota originated in the Black Hills and the sacred instructions given to us by the Creator were given to us on Bear Butte." By making this analogy, Red Shirt locates a point of similarity between Lakota religion, Judaism, Christianity, and Islam. All four religions associate powerful religious experiences with specific mountains. By encouraging Jews, Christians, and Muslims to think of Bear Butte as the Lakota Mt. Sinai, Red Shirt helps Jews, Christians, and Muslims appreciate the respect Lakotas feel for that particular site.

In a given year, four thousand American Indians worship on Bear Butte. One of them was Good Lifeways Woman. While on a vision quest during the 1970s, something remarkable happened. The powers manifested themselves to her:

> I was facing north and fell asleep. In that state I saw a
> large shape approaching me . . . It was so big that it

almost covered the sky. When it got closer I could see
that it was an owl. . . . Soon that owl took on the shape
of a man. . . . The man drew a circle in the dirt. In the
dirt appeared an owl's face and an eagle's face. [A] blue
light asked, 'Are you ready? When you are ready I will
help you.' And that blue light traveled all around me.

Subsequent dreams and visions helped Good Lifeways
Woman become an important healer among her people. Her
experience on Bear Butte transformed her and invigorated the
Lakota people.

Nowadays, this type of experience is threatened by outsiders. One hundred thousand tourists a year visit Bear Butte
State Park, one of the newer parks in the South Dakota system.
Most of them know little or nothing about Native American
religion; some of them make it impossible for Native American
peoples to carry out essential ceremonies. Tourists ride deafen-
ing motorcycles. They play their radios at maximum volume so
everyone can hear their favorite songs. They pester vision seekers and, according to some Lakotas, alienate the spirits. They
remove symbolic offerings to the spirits left by Lakotas, treating
these offerings as "cool" souvenirs. Even tourists who consider
themselves friends of Native Americans can interfere with wor-
shippers' vision quests. These "friends" make noise, intrude on
the seekers' privacy, ask inappropriate questions, take unwanted
photographs and videotapes, and occupy and pollute sites tradi-
tionally used by Native visionaries. These and other non-Native
activities damage Plains Indian spirituality at its fountainhead,
where the individual touches the spirit world on the sacred
mountain. Unfortunately, what is true of Bear Butte is true of
many other Native American sacred sites.

In several Canadian provinces, including British Columbia,

Quebec, and Alberta, a multitude of development projects have threatened burial grounds and other sites crucial to the spiritual lives of Canada's First Peoples. Similarly, the expansion of a ski resort in a national forest on the San Francisco Peaks near Flagstaff, Arizona, damaged the Navajo religious tradition. The construction and traffic made it more difficult for practitioners of this religion to collect holy plants and objects used in rituals. Near Holbrook, Arizona, the mining of a gravel pit for a federal road project obliterated Hopi shrines. In the mountains of eastern Tennessee, the Tennessee Valley Authority built a dam that flooded the ceremonial centers and several burial grounds of the Cherokee people. In Arizona, a new dam created Lake Powell and drowned Rainbow Bridge, a sacred Navajo monument. On Devil's Tower in Wyoming, thousands of recreational climbers interfere with the vision quests of Lakotas and others seeking solitude at this important pilgrimage site.

A conflict involving land in northern California led to an important Supreme Court decision that may allow additional damage to Native sites in the future. At the beginning of the 1980s, the U.S. Forest Service proposed building a road to improve access to timber and recreational resources. Karuk, Yurok, and Tolowa Indians sued, in the case of *Lyng* v. *Northern Indian Cemetery Protective Association*, to prevent the road from being built through what they call "the high country." They explained that this was their holy landscape. Here was the haven of fundamental spirits. Here was the necropolis or resting place for the souls of deceased spiritual leaders. Here was the religious academy where their "doctors" or shamans received their powers and visions. Here was the sanctuary where their priests performed ceremonies essential to the well-being and renewal of the world. This landscape was so vital to their existence as a people that they knew it intimately and had a name for its every feature. Without question, their religion centered on this sacred geography and would be harmed by this road. Their case seemed strong.

In 1988, however, the U.S. Supreme Court ruled against the Indians. The justices decided that because the government (the Forest Service) was not intentionally trying to harm the Indians' religion, the First Amendment provided no support for the Indians' side. The road could be built, even if it would "virtually destroy the Indians' ability to practice their religion." This ruling alarmed the Native American peoples of northern California. Many legal scholars feared that the decision weakened constitutional protections of the religious freedom of all Americans, especially those practicing minority faiths.

Native American religions that survive defeats in court may face other threats to their well-being. Even if a future Court were to reverse the *Lyng* decision, and even if every state were to safeguard Native sacred sites and protect Native religious practices, the long-term security of Native religions would not be guaranteed. The well-being of any religion depends upon the well-being of the communities who hold it. Today many Native communities are ravaged by high levels of illness, bad diets, and poor health care. The statistics stun outsiders. Among Oglala Indians living on Pine Ridge Reservation, for example, 40 percent of women and 50 percent of men have diabetes. American Indians smoke at a higher rate than any other population in the United States. One in three Native men smoke, as do one in four women. Many American Indians die young, victims of suicide, domestic violence, and automobile accidents, at rates two to three times higher than those of other youths. Their deaths cause great pain and rob families and nations of promising leaders, artists, and visionaries. According to the newspaper *News From Indian Country* on the largest reservation in the United States, the Navajo reservation, "unemployment is five times greater, . . . average income is three times lower, teen suicide is twice as high" as the national average and "murder rates are as many as five times those of neighboring counties." Such conditions can breed despair and cynicism, undermine hope and confidence, and sap the spirit of Native American individuals.

Meanwhile, television distracts Native people from age-old communal spiritual paths, pointing them toward consumerism. "TV, that's this generation," Dennis Bedonie, a Navajo peyote leader, asserted to Emily Benedek, a visiting writer. He lamented how television channels the aspirations and bends the values of his teenage children.

Television also affects the linguistic skills of young American Indians. Because it relies almost exclusively upon the English language, television in the United States promotes mastery of English at the expense of Native tongues. As a consequence, Native American youths who lack fluency in their native languages find it more difficult to understand and master chants, songs, prayers, and stories vital to their people's religions. Instead of memorizing oral traditions thousands of years old, they are learning the plots of popular television shows and films. Video games and Internet web sites often reinforce this trend. The shift to English seriously impairs traditional religions.

This latest challenge to Native languages continues a long history of linguistic threat. The contest began the moment

Europeans gained political dominance in America. The cause of Native languages seemed lost during the modern era of boarding schools, where Anglo teachers would beat Native American children for not speaking English exclusively. In spite of these severe challenges, however, many languages survived. Today, in Oklahoma, in some Native American communities elders provide language instruction in day-care centers and schools. In Navajo and Lakota country, radio stations broadcast programs in the languages of the people, using technology to nurture what their ancestors created and sustained.

American Indians also confront psychological challenges. They find themselves stereotyped by non-Natives. This hurts their self-image and can make it difficult for them to win support for their religious freedom. Stereotypes magnify isolated behaviors or traits for the purposes of ridicule or condemnation. The most common stereotype of Native Americans depicts them as doomed, horse-mounted, buffalo-hunting nomads who wore long feathered headdresses, lacked a sense of humor, and roamed the Great Plains looking for settlers to attack. This stereotype shows up in Hollywood Westerns and popular television shows, on tobacco and food product labels, on old coins, album covers, and at sporting events in the form of Indian mascots. The Cleveland Indians symbolize their team with an image of a smiling big-toothed Native man. In Atlanta, Georgia, another major league baseball franchise calls its team the "Braves." This name calls to mind images of Indians as bloodthirsty "savages." And indeed, at Braves games, thousands of fans chop the air with plastic "tomahawks" to express their excitement. These antics elicited strong protest from Native American critics during the 1990s when the Braves played in the World Series, but nothing changed.

A more recent stereotype relates directly to Native American religions. It suggests American Indians are naturally spiritual, as if they lived in a magic realm or distant time unlike those experienced by other human beings. Entranced by this stereotype, many non-Natives now look to American Indians for spiritual insight. To satisfy this hunger a virtual industry has grown up. It includes fake "shamans" who provide weekend retreats to seekers in exchange for cash, a good deal of New Age music featuring Native American chanting and drums, and many books supposedly revealing Native American wisdom to readers. This stereotype, like the others, hurts far more than it helps. Ironically, it leads non-Natives to ignore the real challenges faced by Native religions, including the desecration of their sacred sites.

To be stereotyped in these ways is exhausting, frustrating, and painful for American Indians. Rick Hill, a Tuscarora artist, probes this degrading experience with his photo collage, *Surrounded by Stereotypes*. In the center, the collage features a contemporary Native man wearing jeans and a sports jacket. This image is framed on all sides by standard "Indian" images clipped from advertisements, cartoons, museum exhibits, and Hollywood Westerns. The corners of the collage feature tomahawks. The overall message is that Native people were dangerous natural creatures who lived in the past. The man in the center cradles a beer bottle. Is this another stereotype? Or is the artist suggesting that some contemporary Indian men and women drink to escape the stereotypes that define and defile them?

Stereotypes do psychological and spiritual damage. Confronted with so many images of what Indians are like, young Native people wonder if they are sufficiently Indian. John H. Hunter, a Winnebago/Ojibwa teenager says, "Urban Native youth today have an identity crisis like no other generation before us." Family Services coordinator Elaine Romero of Taos Pueblo in northern New Mexico agrees. "We have a lot of internal struggles, not just within our community but within ourselves." The results can be disastrous. Doctors working with young women addicted to drugs and alcohol find often that they do not feel worthwhile. Many of them doubt their self-worth. In a treatment program for Choctaw women, social workers heal by providing alternative and healthier images of Indianness. Restoring health "involves a spiritual awakening or reawakening" and relies upon Native culture, music, and art. Similarly, at Taos Pueblo, Romero encourages people suffering from substance abuse and depression to reconnect with traditional Pueblo ways: "We have to make time to plant corn, even if it's just a little, to reinstitute what is most perfect in our culture." The illness is not simply physical; the cure must involve cultural and spiritual actions. John Hunter, showing confidence in his generation, says, "Indian youth can and will strengthen their traditional life above the rapidly diversifying city." Far from rendering Native American spirituality obsolete, difficult challenges can deepen people's commitment to religious life.

These healing approaches mirror on a smaller scale what is happening at large among American Indians. Modern Native healers are working to undo the damage caused by old stereotypes and to create better images and lives for young people living in the twenty-first century. Native healers today include a wide range of creative people: elders, storytellers, dancers, medicine people, and priests, but also musicians, artists, politicians, writers, scholars, humorists, lawyers, counselors, health workers, and intellectuals. For example, a popular singer like Buffy Sainte-Marie glories that Native people can thrive in the contemporary world. She eagerly embraces new technologies. "People thought I was out of my mind, even as recently as two years ago, for talking about Indian people and computers. White people were laughing up their sleeves, thinking, 'That's a funny idea.' That was really insulting. I said, 'OK, that does it. I'm writing an article,' so I did. It's called 'Cyberskins' and is on my web site."

Buffy Sainte-Marie, who began as a folk singer, excels in electronic music. Performers such as flutist R. Carlos Nakai, Joy Harjo and Poetic Justice, Ulali, Keith Secola and his Wild Indians, John Trudell and Bad Dog, Joanne Shenandoah, Jim Boyd and the band Indigenous, Robbie Robertson, Kashtin, Chester Knight and the Wind, Lunar Drive, Litefoot, Haida, Walela, and others innovate in jazz, rock, dance beat, rap, and country forms. Sam Minkler, a Navajo who first learned to sing in Black Mesa, Arizona, around a fire in a hogan—a traditional Navajo home—thinks his singing on Lunar Drive albums echoes classic Navajo behavior. Just as his ancestors assimilated new things brought by Europeans into their lives, including sheep and wool, Minkler grafts modern music onto his own singing tradition. Conversely, he brings *Hozhoni*, Navajo spirituality and perspective, to modern music. Everyone comes out the richer for his efforts to reinvent what it means to be an "Indian."

What is true in music is true as well in sculpture, painting, weaving, pottery, basket making, jewelry, photography, and other media. "We are in the midst of the renaissance of Native American art," D. Marisa Huntinghorse, a Wichita, says. "When one thinks about the legacy today's Native American artisans are leaving behind for future generations, it is breathtaking." In art, Native American men and women find creative ways to express religious values, symbols, and experiences. Colleen Cutschall, an Oglala Sicangu Lakota from Pine Ridge, South Dakota, uses acrylic paint to produce large abstract canvases that depict the Lakota creation stories. In one of these stories, a superior god named Inyan helped create the world by letting his blue blood flow out to create the rivers and streams and the blue dome of the sky. Cutschall's painting *Blue Blood* centers on a hand in which blue blood flows, calling to mind Inyan's power in the moment before his great sacrifice. Another Cutschall painting depicts the emergence of the first humans from the womb of the earth.

Spirituality shapes the works of Navajo painter Shonto Begay. His mother, a Navajo weaver, and his father, a Navajo medicine man, taught him to view the world in a religious manner. "We belong to the land," he says, "it does not belong to us, nature is more than just what we see—she is life and therefore gives and maintains life. She commands humility and respect." In his paintings, Begay considers how Navajos reconcile and fail to reconcile traditional values with the realities of modern reservation life.

Meanwhile, many talented Native writers use fiction to illumine a "mixed" life where religions and cultures interact, sometimes clashing, sometimes fusing. Ray A. Young Bear

(Mesquakie) describes a tribal culture that blends traditional mythic figures with characters from *MAD* magazine and famous criminals Bonnie and Clyde. Another author, Leslie Silko, a Laguna Pueblo novelist, enlivens her works by retelling traditional sacred stories in modern settings. In her 1977 novel *Ceremony*, she blends poems, songs, and chants describing supernatural beings with the painful tale of a man named Tayo. Tayo, a war veteran and mixed-blood person, searches for identity and purpose. By the end of the book, the supernatural beings have become real characters, and the war veteran has learned to see the mythic significance within ordinary things. A "ceremony" has healed him and brought new power to his people. Other authors treat similar struggles of Native people contending with racism, alcoholism, and other challenges. They include N. Scott Momaday (Kiowa), James Welch (Blackfoot/Gros Ventre), Luci Tapahonso (Navajo), Louise Erdrich (Turtle Mountain Chippewa), Joy Harjo (Creek), Maurice Kenny (Mohawk), Diane Glancy (Cherokee), Gerald Vizenor (Anishinaabe), Simon Ortiz (Acoma Pueblo), Mary Tall Mountain (Athabascan), Sherman Alexie (Spokane), and many others. This literary outpouring, an unprecedented development in American history, shows no signs of ebbing.

Also unprecedented was a film like *Smoke Signals*. Released commercially in 1998, it was the first major film written, directed, and co-produced by Native Americans. (The film was written, directed, and produced by Sherman Alexie and Chris Eyre [Cheyenne/Arapahoe].) It challenged stereotypes of Indians as silent, humorless, and super-spiritual people. Instead, as Alexie said, *Smoke Signals* showed "some Indians worrying about love, hope, sex and dreams." To help non-Native audiences feel comfortable with the film's reservation context, the film employed some familiar actors, including two from a popular 90s television show, *Northern Exposure*. And, as Alexie acknowledged, the film wrapped its characters "In a frame that everyone recognizes—the roadtrip buddy move" à la *Thelma and Louise*. The buddies here were Thomas Builds-the-Fire, played by Evan Adams (Coast Salish) as a geeky, spiritually attuned young man, and Victor Joseph, played by Adam Beach (Ojibway) as a more jaded, but honorable man in search of the truth about his father. As the film followed these protagonists on their journey, it pondered how parents and children grow apart as well as how they heal severed relationships. A down-to-earth film, it nevertheless raised deep and fundamental questions.

Among Native Americans, making art and telling stories have often fed or followed religious quests. Art emerges from these quests and quickens their pulse as well. So it is not surprising to find art and religion united in the music of Joy Harjo, the paintings of Colleen Cutschall, the novels of Leslie Silko, or films of Chris Eyre. More surprising are the ways contemporary Native men and women turn secular activities toward spiritual ends. Native American lawyers, working along with non-Native lawyers for the Native American Rights Fund, use their expertise to protect sacred sites and threatened religious practices. They have defended peyotists victimized by drug laws, helped prisoners prevented from participating in sweat-lodge ceremonies, spoken for tribal members arrested for possession of eagle feathers—sacred to Indians, but protected by the federal government—and aided tribal communities seeking to reassert ancestral treaty rights and resume political sovereignty. Siding with David against Goliath, the lawyers do not always win in their attempts to defend Native religions, but their dedication and intelligence improve the odds.

Money helps too. One of the fastest-growing industries in Indian country is tourism. It benefits White Mountain Apaches, who run a profitable world-class ski resort near Fort Apache, Arizona. Similarly, nineteen tribes of Pueblo Indians in New Mexico own and operate the Indian Pueblo Cultural Center, an attractive facility in Albuquerque. "Be-po-wa-ve," which means "welcome" in Tewa, is the message it conveys to outsiders. Here visitors can contemplate informative exhibits in an excellent Native-designed museum, eat traditional Native American foods in the restaurant, shop for sandpaintings and kachina dolls in the gift shop, and observe Taos dancers performing in a centrally located plaza. Still other groups are attracting tourists by sponsoring rodeos, powwows, and art fairs, and by marketing their beautiful natural landscapes. These ventures, however, carry some risks. As Faith Roessel, a Navajo and Special Assistant to the U.S. Secretary of the Interior explains, unchecked tourism, traffic, and economic development can disturb the balance of people with their land. She has seen how Monument Valley, on the Navajo reservation at the border of Arizona and Utah, has become a favorite location for advertisers. "I turn on the TV and see Madison Avenue is peddling yet another product with the stark, red buttes of Monument Valley as a backdrop . . . I feel ambivalent about this, proud of my people and land, yet not wanting its uniqueness and sacredness marred by outsiders." Tourism provides mixed blessings, even when Native entrepreneurs profit.

Far more destructive, however, is another enterprise common in Indian country: the leasing of tribal lands for toxic dumps. Such deals, in spite of the money they produce, evoke anger from tribal members. When some Mescalero Apache leaders planned to use tribal land to build a storage facility for the radioactive waste from U.S. nuclear power plants, a deep rift developed among tribal members. Many desired the income such a facility would produce. Others believed such usage contradicted the land's holiness.

During the 1990s, nearly two hundred Native nations sought a strong financial base by running casinos. Cleaner than toxic dumps, casinos proved controversial and lucrative. A $2.6-billion industry in 1993 and a $6-billion one in 1997, Indian gaming enriched the Mashantucket Pequot, the Shakopee Mdewakanton Dakota, the Oneida of Wisconsin, and the Sycuan Mission Indians. The Pequot did so well they returned $500,000 in housing aid to the federal government and suggested the money go to poorer tribes. Other groups did not achieve that level of success, but enjoyed the profits gambling provides. In 1996, casinos among Pueblo tribes in New Mexico employed 4,275 people and produced profits of $260 million.

With so much money moving through tribal casinos, inevitably a few individuals here and there did not behave well. Some came to resemble the fictional characters described in Ray A. Young Bear's novel *Remnants of the First Earth* as "money-hungry piranhas on a wild feeding frenzy." Their example dismayed many and may explain why in 1994 Navajos voted not to introduce gambling to their reservation. By a margin of five thousand votes they rejected an industry that would have produced annual profits of $60 million.

In spite of these problems, however, most tribes involved in gaming seemed to feel the good outweighed the bad. Casinos provided jobs where they were most needed. On some reservations, casinos became so essential tribal leaders dubbed them "the new buffalo." Just as the Plains Indians once depended upon the great bison for their daily needs, so some contemporary Indians depend upon casinos for their livelihood. Gaming profits funded improvements in educational facilities and supported new social programs for children and elders. In an interesting twist, some tribal governments found ways to use the "new buffalo" to reinvigorate ancestral values. Using proceeds from two Idaho casinos, Nez Percé Indians built up a herd of Appaloosa horses, the breed developed by their ancestors, and bought land for a wildlife refuge and restocked it with wolves, animals sacred to many Native peoples. In 1997, the Nez Percé bought ten thousand acres of land in the Wallowa Valley in Oregon. The land was associated with their most famous leader, Chief Joseph, a man who was forced to abandon it more than a century ago, never to return. Tribal elder Horace Axtell, a descendant of Chief Joseph, renamed the area "Precious Land." Thus, casino profits helped the Nez Percé heal a wound from U.S. history and will enable future generations of Nez Percé to reconnect with their people's treasured landscape.

Other acts of healing resemble the Nez Percé example. In the 1990s, Anishinaabe people, with money raised through the White Earth Land Recovery Project, purchased ancestral lands in Minnesota. They grow wild rice and other traditional crops there to maintain continuity between past, present, and future generations. Meanwhile, the Nambe Pueblo people, through the Intertribal Bison Cooperative, restored buffalo to their New Mexican landscape. They viewed this event as "a welcomed homecoming for the Nambe tribe. The grazing herd of twenty-one buffalo will be used to educate the young, enhance tribal unity, and instill Native values of respect, harmony, and understanding." As these and many other examples suggest, when Native peoples have the power to do so, many of them seek to strengthen their traditions. They repair what colonialism has harmed, restoring the lands and symbols essential to their spiritualities and identities.

Poised between past generations and conscious of future ones, contemporary American Indians continue to change the course of American history. Many of them seek to reverse the currents of destruction and speed those of rejuvenation. Across North America, they work to regain land, retrieve tribal artifacts housed in museums, and rebury their ancestral dead. During recent decades, they have experienced many setbacks, but also some important successes. For example, in 1970, the people of Taos Pueblo regained Blue Lake, their most sacred shrine. Another success came in 1980 when the Zunis persuaded the Smithsonian Institution to return to them the *Ahayuida*, sacred statues of war gods. These statues had been stolen from the Zuni people. In a significant and moving ceremony, museum personnel delivered the statues to Zuni religious leaders. The Zunis placed the statues in a protected space where they could decompose and return to the earth. With the support of the U.S. Justice Department, the Zunis have regained control over dozens of *Ahayuida* from collectors and auction houses. Every return of a war god completes a ritual cycle long delayed, correcting yet another historic wrong.

Additional healing will happen as Indian peoples invoke an important law passed by Congress in 1990. The Native American Graves and Repatriation Act (NAGPRA) "recognizes

the human rights of Indians," and restores to them their property rights, "in terms of communal objects." According to
Richard Hill, Sr., a Tuscarora scholar, the Act "ends a pattern of
one-way transfer of objects from Indian hands to non-Indian
institutions." Thanks to the Act, Indians can now require museums and other institutions to inventory their Native holdings
and return artifacts improperly acquired. Many of these objects
have religious significance. Indeed, to many Native people such
things as eagle feathers, ceremonial masks, and human skeletons
are not "objects" at all, but living spiritual entities. Many Native
Americans feel these entities need to be released from stone
buildings, repatriated or brought home, and cared for in traditional ways. Repatriation involves the legal system and scientific
museums, but for Native peoples it touches sacred matters as
well. Suzan Shown Harjo (Cheyenne and Hodulgee Muscogee)
portrays repatriation as a "settling of spirits" that enables Native
people to meet and gain "spiritual knowledge and comfort from
sacred beings." Freeing the spirits from museums, Native
Americans fortify themselves and invigorate their cultural traditions.

In the world of museums, repatriation is big news for cura-
tors and good news for American Indians. The best news, however, may be the building and opening of the new National
Museum of the American Indian. Part of the Smithsonian
Institution, this museum occupies the last site remaining open
on the Mall in Washington, D.C. The Mall is the symbolic center of the United States, the place where Americans go to learn
what it means to be an American. Some would call it a sacred
place. By locating a new National Museum of the American
Indian there, the U.S. government and all the people who

helped pay for it recognize the historic, enduring, and eternal presence of Native American peoples in North America. Designed by a team of Native and non-Native architects and directed by W. Richard West (Cheyenne), this museum is scheduled to open in 2002. According to the museum's web site, it will work "in collaboration with the Native peoples of the Western Hemisphere to protect and foster their cultures by reaffirming traditions and beliefs, encouraging contemporary artistic expression, and empowering the Indian voice." The involvement of American Indians at every stage of the project represents a fundamentally new approach to museology. What the film *Smoke Signals* was to cinema, this museum may be to national halls of memory. Like the film, its existence suggests contemporary Indians are gaining greater control over how they are represented. And it nurtures the hope that the new museum will succeed in changing forever and for the better how all Americans view American Indians. Only time will tell.

Also uncertain is the future of Native American religions. Various prospects coincide. On the dark side, Native religions are threatened by many forces, some old, some new. And some, like old stereotypes broadcast on the new medium of television, blend old and new in potent and toxic ways. To be sure, things are not as bad as they were during the latter part of the nineteenth century or the first half of the twentieth. No longer are major Native religions outlawed. No longer are Native children stripped from their families and forced to attend Christian boarding schools. No longer is federal Indian policy designed to crush Native cultures. However, if the darkest time has passed, it is not all sunshine and light either. Prejudices against Native religions continue to thrive among non-Native populations;

state and federal officials continue to make decisions harmful to Native religious life; and larger economic and social patterns continue to affect Native communities in destructive ways. Additionally, novel threats to Indian religions have appeared and gained force in recent decades. The media-driven spread of the English language and the decline of tribal ones presents an unprecedented challenge. On the other hand, an equally unprecedented renaissance of art, music, and literature crafted by Native artists, musicians, and writers may sow the seeds of cultural renewal. In sum, it is unlikely the twenty-first century will bring the demise of Native American religions, languages, and peoples, but it will not witness the rebirth of all of them either.

As the third millennium unfolds, for Native America it is neither nadir nor nirvana. Not all of their religious practices will persist, and few will elude serious challenges, but many of the most important ones will continue to shape and inspire the lives of American Indians. And, as always, new songs and new visions will transform American Indians and their religions. Together with the tested traditions, these new songs and visions will help American Indians to survive even when the odds say they should not, and perhaps their religions to thrive in ways impossible to anticipate.

CHRONOLOGY

3000 BCE
American Indians construct a mound complex in the lower Mississippi Valley near present-day Monroe, Louisiana

1000 BCE
American Indians intensify production of domesticated crops

300 CE
Hopewellian communities complete construction of grand buildings and the Fairgrounds Circle near Newark, Ohio; their design employs symbols associated with the Earth-Diver creation story

1150
Hopis found Old Oraibi and Acoma villages on mesas in Arizona; 850 years later they remained inhabited, making them the oldest continuously inhabited towns in North America

1200
The great town of Cahokia flourishes near the Mississippi River, across from the present-day location of St. Louis, Missouri

Anasazi Pueblo civilization thrives in Colorado and New Mexico

1400
In central Mexico, the Aztec city Tenochtitlán involves 250,000 people directly and constitutes one of the largest urban centers in the world

1400s
Under the guidance of the Peacemaker, a spiritual leader, the Iroquois peoples in the New York region unite as the Hodenosaunee, "the people of the Longhouse," in a Great League of Peace and Power

1520

Spanish invaders conquer Tenochtitlán and destroy Aztec temples

1540

Mound-building, town-dwelling agriculturalists in the Southeast and Zunis and other Pueblo peoples in the Southwest resist the invasion of their land by Spanish armies searching for gold

16TH–20TH century

Successive epidemics of diseases introduced by Europeans—measles, small pox, chicken pox, influenza, mumps, typhus, cholera, and whooping cough—kill millions of Native American men, women, and children

1675

Massachuset Indians abandon "praying towns," segregated communities established by an English minister to promote Christianity among them

1751

A Delaware prophetess in Pennsylvania warns her people not to adopt Christianity

1762

Pontiac, aided by the prophet Neolin, leads many Native nations in the Ohio Valley in a massive anti-British uprising

1799

Seneca visionary Handsome Lake teaches the Gaiwiiyo, or the Good Word, a moral code that strengthens Iroquois culture

1804

Shawnee prophet Tenskwatawa, "the Open Door," receives his first great vision; with his brother Tecumseh, he leads a pan-Indian movement opposed to alcohol abuse, dependence upon European commerce, and the loss of Native lands to the United States

1814

On March 27, at the Battle of Horseshoe Bend in Alabama, Creek Indian rebels, led by prophets, suffer devastating losses fighting an army of U.S. soldiers, Cherokees, and other Creeks

1817

New England Protestant missionaries establish Brainerd, a boarding school for Cherokee youth, in Tennessee

1820s–1840s

The United States forces whole nations of Native peoples, including Cherokees, Creeks, Choctaws, Seminoles, Ottawas, Miamis, and Shawnees, to leave their homelands in the East and move to Oklahoma, Kansas, and Iowa. Their land becomes the basis for several new states, and in the Southeast their removal makes possible the rapid expansion of cotton agriculture and the spread of African American slavery, a cause of the American Civil War

1876

Lakota and Cheyenne people defeat the U.S. Cavalry at Greasy Grass in the Battle of Little Big Horn

late 19TH–mid 20TH century

U.S. policies and laws forbid the practice of many Native American religions and religious practices. U.S. officials separate Native children from their parents and place them in boarding schools where they are forced to learn English, Christianity, and non-Native values.

1877

Quanah Parker, Comanche warrior, rancher, and businessman in Texas and Oklahoma, encounters the peyote religion for the first time. He becomes its foremost champion among the Comanches.

1880s

Buffalo, once numbering in the tens of millions and central to the religious life of Plains Indian peoples, are brought to the brink of extinction by Anglo hunters

1889

Wovoka, a Tövusidökadö Pauite Indian of Mason Valley, Nevada, receives a powerful vision of a dance that promises to reunite the living and the dead and to uncover a joyous world for American Indians

1890

Lakotas of the northern Plains develop their own version of Wovoka's new religion and dance the "Ghost Dance." On December 29, a U.S. army massacres 200 Lakota men, women, and children at Wounded Knee, South Dakota

1918

Oklahoma peyotists organize the Native American Church to promote "the Christian religion with the practice of the Peyote Sacrament"

1970

The Taos Pueblo people of New Mexico regain control of Blue Lake, their most sacred shrine

1980

Museums begin returning to the Zunis of New Mexico the *Ahayuida*, sacred statues of war gods stolen from the Zunis in the past

1988

The U.S. Supreme Court decides in the case of *Lyng v. Northern Indian Cemetery Protective Association* that the U.S. Forest Service can build a road in northern California, even though it would virtually destroy the ability of Karuk, Yurok, and Tolowa Indians to practice their religion

1989

Visions inspire Ola Cassadore Davis to form the Apache Survival Coalition, an alliance of Native American and non-Native environmentalists, to fight the construction of a new observatory on Dzil Nchaa Si An (Mt. Graham in Arizona), a sacred mountain

1990

Congress passes the Native American Graves and Repatriation Act, which recognizes the human rights of Indians and restores to them property rights in terms of communal objects, including human remains, eagle feathers, ceremonial objects, and other sacred entities

1994

Navajos, who comprise the largest tribe in the United States, vote against introducing casino gambling to their reservation

2002

The National Museum of the American Indian, part of the Smithsonian Institution is due to open on the last available site on the Mall in Washington, D.C. It reaffirms Native traditions and beliefs while helping to change for the better how all Americans view Indians.

FURTHER READING

WORKS FOCUSED ON THE PAST

Calloway, Colin G., ed., *Our Hearts Fell to the Ground: Plains Indian Views of How the West Was Lost.* Boston: Bedford Books, 1996.

Clendinnen, Inga. *Aztecs: An Interpretation.* Cambridge and New York: Cambridge University Press, 1991.

DeMallie, Raymond J., ed. *The Sixth Grandfather: Black Elk's Teachings Given to John G. Neihardt.* Lincoln: University of Nebraska Press, 1984.

Dowd, Gregory Evans. *A Spirited Resistance: The North American Struggle for Unity, 1745–1815.* Baltimore: Johns Hopkins University Press, 1992.

Heckwelder, John. *History, Manners, and Customs of the Indian Nations Who Once Inhabited Pennsylvania and the Neighboring States.* 1876. Reprint, New York: Arno Press, 1971.

Kennedy, Roger G. *Hidden Cities: The Discovery and Loss of Ancient North American Civilization.* New York: Penguin, 1994.

Martin, Joel W. *Sacred Revolt: The Muskogees' Struggle for a New World.* Boston: Beacon Press, 1991.

McLoughlin, William G. *Cherokees and Missionaries, 1789–1839.* New Haven: Yale University Press, 1984.

O'Connell, Barry, ed. *On Our Own Ground: The Complete Writings of William Apess, a Pequot.* Amherst: University of Massachusetts Press, 1992.

Thornton, Russell. *American Indian Holocaust and Survival: A Population History Since 1492.* Norman: University of Oklahoma Press, 1987.

Vecsey, Christopher. *On the Padres' Trails.* Notre Dame, Ind.: University of Notre Dame Press, 1996.

Wallace, Anthony F. C. *The Death and Rebirth of the Seneca.* New York: Vintage, 1969.

WORKS FOCUSED ON SPECIFIC TRADITIONS OR PEOPLES

Basso, Keith H. *Wisdom Sits in Places: Landscape and Language among the Western Apache.* Albuquerque: University of New Mexico Press, 1996.

Bierhorst, John. *Mythology of the Lenape: Guide and Texts.* Tucson: University of Arizona Press, 1995.

Brightman, Robert. *Grateful Prey: Rock Cree Human-Animal Relationships.* Berkeley: University of California Press, 1993.

Hudson, Charles. *The Southeastern Indians.* Knoxville: University of Tennessee Press, 1976.

Irwin, Lee. *The Dreamseekers: Native American Visionary Traditions of the Great Plains.* Norman: University of Oklahoma Press, 1994.

Nelson, Richard K. *Make Prayers to the Raven: A Koyukon View of the Northern Forest.* Chicago: University of Chicago Press, 1983.

St. Pierre, Mark, and Tilda Long Soldier. *Walking in a Sacred Manner: Healers, Dreamers, and Pipe Carriers—Medicine Women of the Plains Indians.* New York: Simon & Schuster, 1995.

Walker, James R. *Lakota Belief and Ritual.* Ed. Raymond J. DeMallie and Elaine Jahner. Lincoln: University of Nebraska Press, 1980.

GHOST DANCE AND PEYOTE RELIGION

Aberle, David. *The Peyote Religion Among the Navaho.* Norman: University of Oklahoma Press, 1991.

Hagan, William T. *Quanah Parker, Comanche Chief.* Norman: University of Oklahoma Press, 1993.

Hittman, Michael. *Wovoka and the Ghost Dance: A Sourcebook.* Carson City, Nev.: Grace Dangberg, 1990.

Kehoe, Alice Beck. *The Ghost Dance: Ethnohistory and Revitalization.* Fort Worth, Tex.: Holt, Rinehart, and Winston, 1989.

Mooney, James. *The Ghost-Dance Religion and Wounded Knee.* 1896. Reprint, New York: Dover, 1973.

Stewart, Omer. *Peyote Religion: A History.* Norman: University of Oklahoma Press, 1987.

Vander, Judith. *Shoshone Ghost Dance Religion: Poetry Songs and Great Basin Context.* Urbana: University of Illinois Press, 1997.

RESPONDING TO MODERN LIFE

Benedek, Emily. *Beyond the Four Corners of the World: A Navajo Woman's Journey.* New York: Knopf, 1995.

Frazier, Ian. *On the Rez.* New York: Farrar, Straus & Giroux, 2000.

Loftin, John D. *Religion and Hopi Life in the Twentieth Century.* Bloomington: Indiana University Press, 1991.

McNally, Michael D. *Ojibwe Singers: Hymns, Grief, and a Native Culture in Motion.* New York: Oxford University Press, 2000.

Northrup, Jim. *Walking the Rez Road.* Stillwater, Minn.: Voyageur Press, 1993.

RELIGIOUS THOUGHT AND EXPRESSION

Deloria, Vine, Jr. *For This Land: Writings on Religion in America.* New York: Routledge, 1999.

Deloria, Vine, Jr. *God is Red: A Native View of Religion.* 2nd ed. Golden, Colo.: North American Press, 1992

Harjo, Joy. *The Spiral of Memory: Interviews.* Edited by Laura Coltelli. Ann Arbor: University of Michigan Press, 1996.

Lankford, George, ed. and comp. *Native American Legends, Southeastern Legends: Tales from the Natchez, Caddo, Biloxi, Chickasaw, and Other Nations.* Little Rock, Ark.: August House, 1987.

Marshall, Ann. *Rain: Native Expressions from the American Southwest.* Santa Fe: Museum of New Mexico Press, 2000.

Nabokov, Peter, and Robert Easton. *Native American*

Architecture. New York: Oxford University Press, 1989.

Pflüg, Melissa A. *Ritual and Myth In Odawa Revitalization: Reclaiming a Sovereign Place.* Norman: University of Oklahoma Press, 1998.

Treat, James, ed. *Native and Christian: Indigenous Voices on Religious Identity in the United States and Canada.* New York: Routledge, 1996.

Vecsey, Christopher. *Imagine Ourselves Richly: Mythic Narratives of North American Indians.* New York: Crossroad, 1988.

Williamson, Ray A., and Claire R. Farrer, eds. *Earth and Sky: Native American Cosmovision.* Albuquerque: University of New Mexico Press, 1993.

CONTESTING NON-NATIVE FORCES AND STEREOTYPES

Bordewich, Fergus M. *Killing the White Man's Indian: Reinventing Native Americans at the End of the Twentieth Century.* New York: Anchor, 1996.

Churchill, Ward. *Fantasies of the Master Race: Literature, Cinema, and the Colonization of the American Indian.* Monroe, Maine: Common Courage Press, 1992.

Deloria, Philip J. *Playing Indian.* New Haven: Yale University Press, 1998.

Meister, Barbara, ed. *Mending the Circle: A Native American Repatriation Guide.* New York: The American Indian Ritual Object Repatriation Foundation, 1996.

Taylor, Bron. "Resacralizing Earth: Pagan Environmentalism and the Restoration of Turtle Island," in David Chidester and Edward T. Linenthal, eds., *American Sacred Space.* Bloomington: Indiana University Press, 1995: 97–152.

Thomas, David Hurst. *Skull Wars: Kennewick Man, Archaeology, and the Battle for Native American Identity.* New York: Basic Books, 2000.

Tinker, George E. *Missionary Conquest: The Gospel and Native American Cultural Genocide.* Minneapolis: Fortress Press, 1993.

INDEX

ACKNOWLEDGMENTS

In the course of writing this book, I have learned a great deal, not the least of which is the fact that I have an infinite amount more to learn. The field of Native American religious history is far too big for one person to grasp, let alone for a single book to represent. If I have dared to try to write such an inevitably incomplete book, friends and family deserve some of the credit for encouraging me. Their delightful children—Allen, Melanie, Caroline, Eleanor, Evelyn, Marie, Frank, Robert, Evelyn (again!), and, just in time for the press, Jimmy—made me glad to be writing a book for the next generation. Meanwhile, my parents, as always, inspired me by their admirable example to do my best. My uncle John Martin helped me find Quanah Parker's "Star House" in rural Oklahoma. Zeke, a very good dog, reminded me daily of the world beyond books, and Lisa, a very good human being, made everything a lot more interesting. Without them, I never would have completed this Quixotic project.

It began years ago when Jon Butler invited me to write a book for this series, which features distinguished scholars whom I admire. To me this was the equivalent of getting called up from a Triple A baseball team to play in the major leagues. If I pull my weight, it is due in large part to the support I have received from fine institutions and scholars. I thank the Office of the Dean of Franklin and Marshall College for numerous grants to enhance my teaching, to fund research and travel, and to make possible a sabbatical year of intensive reading and writing. Princeton University's Center for the Study of American Religion and Culture also helped significantly by naming me a Fellow for a year, as did the National Endowment for the Humanities.

Critical help came from archivists and librarians across the county, including those at Princeton University, Princeton Theological Seminary, Colgate-Rochester Seminary, the University of North Carolina at Chapel Hill, Duke University, Harvard University, and the Departments of Archives and History in Oklahoma and Alabama. I thank the Houghton Library of Harvard University for permission to quote from their archival collections related to historic Cherokees. I also thank the many tribal officials, artists, tour guides, and friends living in Creek, Cherokee, Lakota, Hopi, Navajo, and Pueblo communities for their warm hospitality and invaluable perspectives on Native American life.

Jon Butler, Nancy Toff, Michael McNally, and Lisa Barnett read and critiqued the entire text. Many others responded to my ideas and shared their perspectives on writing and teaching about Native American history, literature, and religions. These include Chris Jocks, Michelene Pesantubbee, Ann Morrison Spinney, Mary Churchill, Anita Kline, Gary Larson, Cheryl Walker, John Grim, Lee Irwin, David Hackett, Thomas Tweed, Jace Weaver, David Carrasco, Inés Talamantez, Joy Harjo, Kimberly Blaeser, Leonard Bruguier, the late John Andrew III, members of the Harvard Conference on Indigenous Religions and Ecology, members of the Young Scholars of American Religion and Culture, members of the Lancaster Quest program, members of the Auburn Lifelong Learning program, members of the Haverford NEH Seminar on American Religious Diversity, and members of the Rockefeller Foundation's "Changing Role of Religion and American Life" group. In telling this large story, I also relied heavily upon the exemplary studies of specific communities and themes authored by Keith Basso, Richard Nelson, Melissa Pflüg, Christopher Vecsey, Bron Taylor, James Treat, Lee Irwin, Omer Stewart, Raymond DeMallie, Judith Vander, Alice Kehoe, the late William McLoughlin, and others.

If I have overlooked anyone, I apologize in advance. I doubt that I could ever adequately thank all who have helped me on my way. The book may be finished, but my acknowledgments can never truly end.

TEXT CREDITS

The sidebars in this volume contain extracts of historical documents. Source information on sidebars is as follows:

"The Navajo Creation Story," p. 30: Jerrold E. Levy, *In the Beginning: The Navajo Genesis* (Berkeley: University of California Press, 1998). Reproduced by permission of the Regents of the University of California. © 1998.

"The Seer," p. 59: William Bartram, *The Travels of William Bartram* (New York: Penguin, 1998).

"Catholic Indian/Indian Catholic," p. 83: James Treat, ed., *Native and Christian: Indigenous Voices on Religious Identity in the United States and Canada* (New York: Routledge, 1995). Reproduced by permission of Routledge, Inc. © 1996.

"Peyote Cures Drunkenness," p. 111: "James Mooney and Fracis La Flesche (Omaha) Testify about Peyote, 1918," Albert Hurtado and Peter Iverson, *Major Problems in American Indian History: Documents and Essays* (Lexington, Mass.: D. C. Heath and Company, 1994).

ART CREDITS

Fig. 1: Philadelphia Museum of Art: Purchased with funds from the American Museum of Photography; Fig. 2: Courtesy of the Museum of New Mexico, Neg. No. 57774; Fig. 3: No. 316397, Photo. Wanamaker, Courtesy Dept. of Library Services, American Museum of Natural History; Fig. 4: Ohio Historical Society; Fig. 5: Smithsonian Institution; Fig. 6: Gift of Anne Evans and Mary Kent Wallace, Denver Art Museum; Fig. 7: Library of Congress, Prints & Photographs Division (903026); Fig. 9: Smithsonian Institution; Fig. 10: Library of Congress, Prints & Photographs Divisions (LC-USZ62-094089); Fig. 11: National Museum of Natural History, Smithsonian Institution.

ABOUT THE AUTHOR

After attending public schools in Opelika, Alabama, during the 1960s and '70s, **Joel W. Martin** graduated from Birmingham-Southern College and went on to study in Germany and at Harvard and Duke Universities. His book *Sacred Revolt* (1991) was named an outstanding book on the subject of human rights by the Gustavus Myers Center for the Study of Human Rights. The author of several other publications, he also co-edited *Screening the Sacred: Religion, Myth, and Ideology in Popular American Film* (1995). Martin is the Costo Endowed Chair in American Indian History and Professor in the Departments of History and Religious Studies at the University of California, Riverside.